FAITH, HOPE, AND...
JOY!

The Weapons on Our Belt of Truth

D1464456

Margaret Pogin

ISBN 979-8-88644-457-5 (Paperback)
ISBN 979-8-88644-458-2 (Digital)

Quotes from the Bible, unless noted otherwise, are taken from the New King James Version, copyright © 1982 by Thomas Nelson, Inc. Used by permission. All rights reserved. Scriptures marked ONM are taken from One New Man Bible, © 2011 edited and translated by William J. Morford. Used by permission of True Potential Publishing, Inc.

Covenant Books
11661 Hwy 707
Murrells Inlet, SC 29576
www.covenantbooks.com

What is one of the greatest fears that we all face: Will God provide for me? Margaret's book, *Faith, Hope, and... Joy!* was an encouragement to me. This book was birthed from the teachings she did on the frontlines of the mission field. Our ministry has conducted many Women of Faith, Hope & Joy conferences in Asia, of which Margaret has been a pivotal part, speaking into the lives of the women in attendance. Be prepared to be challenged as you read her words: *Only God is in the business of changing hearts.* Reading these pages, you will gain a deeper understanding of who you are and the importance of your place in this world.

The study on our defensive and offensive weapons is a valuable reminder as we navigate our Christian walk. One of keys to experiencing joy is to cultivate the habit of thankfulness. You will read of Margaret sharing testimonies of His faithfulness. We want a fruitful outcome and to harvest stronger faith, more hope, and abundant joy. We need to also expose our minds to God's word. Our faith cannot grow without the soil of God's word. The living word of God is the greatest tool we have with us, but we often neglect to use this gift. Joy is experienced by communing with God through prayer and by abiding in Christ through God's word.

Margaret is known on the frontlines of our ministry as Mamma Margaret. Mamma Margaret is a woman who exemplifies the virtues in the title of her book. She has a consuming desire to please the Lord Jesus Christ and help equip others.

Thank you, Margaret, for shining the light of truth through this book and encouraging us to believe in His promises so that we can be full of faith, hope, and joy. We are reminded throughout the scriptures that hope is never lost. "Let us hold unswervingly to the hope we profess, for He who promised is faithful," says Hebrews 10:23. During these days, we cling to that promise more than ever.

—Brother Bennie
President and CEO
AlphaMinistries.com
Alpha Bible Churches Asia

This book is very encouraging! Margaret Pogin's book *Faith, Hope, and... Joy!* offers fresh insight and a unique perspective of the application of biblical principles to everyday life. Rather than serving merely as a thesis of theological concepts, the work offers pragmatic and down-to-earth ideas that are deeply rooted in ancient culture and passages. I love that she does not begin at the typical culturally accepted starting points of the dialogue: she is willing to challenge conventional thinking. The results are innovative and refreshing! You will certainly be challenged to grow in how you process biblical spirituality.

—Rev. Rick Whitter
Bishop, Church of God

I learned a long time ago that if you believe in something and decide to pursue it, you must do it with gusto. As you read Margaret Pogin's book, you will witness what *gusto* means. Margaret has captured her passion in the pages of this book and has brought forth in clarity what she believes are the essential tools for every believer. In the end, you will be forced to answer her question for your walk, "What's on your belt?"

—Pastor Keith Johnson
Founder
Biblical Foundations Academy International

For though we walk in the flesh we are not serving as soldiers according to the flesh, for the weapons of our warfare are not fleshly but powerful in God for the tearing down of strongholds, tearing down reasonings even every high thing being lifted up against the knowledge of God, and taking captive every thought in obedience to Messiah, and being ready to punish every disobedience, when your obedience would be achieved.

—2 Corinthians 10:3–6
(One New Man Bible)

CONTENTS

AUTHOR'S NOTE

I purposely chose to use present tense for some of the Bible verses I quote, such as "Jesus says…" or "The Bible says…" I believe that Jesus is still speaking to me, and to us, today. While His words were recorded as being spoken to others over two thousand years ago and, thus, should be past tense (Jesus said…). I believe His words are still relevant and personal to me too. God still talks to us today. The main way for Him to do so is through His Word. So to indicate this, I use present tense in certain places in this book rather than the grammatically correct past tense.

I also vary between using the name Jesus and Y'shua, which is His name in Hebrew. My name is Margaret. When I was taking foreign language classes, I had to choose a name in the language we were studying, but that wasn't really my name. In one case, it would have been the equivalent of my name in that language. In the other language, it was a name of that language that had no correlation to my name. Even with the foreign language names, my real name was still Margaret. That's what is on my birth certificate and what my parents named me. It is what all my friends, teachers, employers, and everyone called me. Jesus is the English name for our Savior, but His name really is Y'shua. I alternate between the two for the sake of getting you familiar with His real Hebrew name, but hopefully not alienating those who had never known this before.

I also intentionally say "Holy Spirit" instead of "the Holy Spirit." Holy Spirit is the third *person* of the Trinity, not just an ethereal foggy substance.

Even with faith, and obedience, and utilizing all the tools you are guided by your Father in heaven to use, sometimes things don't go according to our hopes and plans. This does not mean you have failed. It does mean there are other things Daddy wants to teach you. I do not intend that anyone feel condemnation or guilt when "bad things" continue to happen in our lives. I can assure you God is still with you, and He is in the midst of whatever mess you happen to find yourself in.

From now on, you must right away become strong in *the* Lord and in the power of His strength. You must continually be clothed with the full armor of God to enable you to stand against the strategies of the devil: because the wrestling for us is not with blood and flesh, but with the rulers, with the powers, with the world rulers of this darkness, with the spiritual *forces* of wickedness in the heavenlies. Because of this you must immediately take up the full armor of God, so that you would be able to resist in the evil day and when you have completely achieved all things, to stand. Therefore you should stand, after you have girded around your waist the belt of truth and have put on the breastplate of righteousness and have put sandals on your feet in preparation for the gospel of peace, in all things having taken up the long shield of faith, with which you have been enabled to extinguish all the burning arrows of the evil one: and you must immediately take up the helmet of salvation and the sword of the Spirit, which is the Word of God.

—Ephesians 6:10–17
(One New Man Bible)

1

Boot Camp: Training to Be a Soldier

My best friend, Pat, was diagnosed with colon cancer several years ago. We prayed together. I prayed. Others prayed. When I was able, I went to her home and prayed with her or brought her something to eat when she lost her appetite due to the chemotherapy or took her to doctor appointments. Throughout the entire process, I prayed what she wanted me to pray. When the chemotherapy was finished, she had surgery to remove the tumor and thus part of the large colon. It was there that the doctors discovered cancer cells sprayed all over her blood vessels and other tissue. We continued to pray and believe for healing. The last time I saw her, she was standing at the door to her house. I had dropped her off after taking her to lunch and the grocery store. I hugged her goodbye and told her I loved her, just like usual. She looked at me as I was about to pull out of her driveway and said, "Next time you see me, I'll be looking fantastic." She said that because I was leaving for months and wouldn't see her for a while. I felt a tiny nudge from Holy Spirit to go hug her again, like this would be the last time I saw her. I immediately rejected that thought, thinking it was my doubt sneaking in since we were agreeing together for a miracle of healing. She wound up in the hospital, and I was praying long distance via phone with her daughter-in-law for that miracle of healing. The daughter-in-law said the nurse came to get her and she had to go, so I said I would keep on praying for her. Within an hour, Pat died.

I was in shock. I was crushed. I sobbed. I was so discouraged. I wrote an email to my pastor. I doubted my ability to pray. I doubted the effectiveness of my prayers. I doubted my ability to even hear God. My pastor wrote a very encouraging email back to me. It wasn't any earth-shattering theological teaching on why bad things happen, it was just encouragement to me.

I was sobbing during church the following Sunday (only a few days after Pat's death) when God asked me to list all the things I learned from this experience. I immediately sat down and started that list during the worship. Here's that list:

1. If I had known the future (that Pat would die), I would not have been able to encourage Pat and her family like I did. I do not have that much guile.
2. I still stand on His Word. God heals. I've experienced it. (God miraculously healed me of pernicious anemia.) I know others who have experienced God's healing too. I believe it. I won't change my theology to fit my bad experience.
3. Jesus is real.
4. Jesus loves us so very much. The hardest part for Him was not going to the cross and dying for us, it is right now. The hardest part for Him is the waiting for the Father to say, "Yes, Son, You can go get Your Bride now." He is anxiously awaiting the time when we can be together with Him for eternity—waiting for the marriage supper of The Lamb with His bride—all who believe in Jesus.
5. God is real and personal. Pat isn't just "in heaven" like she arrived "in Paris." She is sitting in the lap of our Father who is loving her like she really deserves.
6. Life is precious and short.
7. Encouragement of others is critical. Pastor's encouragement to me when I doubted all my abilities was so comforting and precious to me.
8. Unless a seed falls to the ground and dies… We don't like this, but it is in Scripture. We need to examine what and why we believe. We really never stop learning. My desire is

to know God more intimately, hear clearer, obey sooner, and understand more so I can help people better.

Through this list, I learned that I had learned a lot. I learned to pray what the person asking for your prayer wants you to pray. I cannot impose and pray my will over theirs. That does not honor them and is not effective. I learned that there is an appointed time for everyone to die. That is in Scripture. I cannot change that.

I also reconfirmed that God talks to us. We need to take the time to fully listen, asking Him for clarification and confirmation, and then allowing time for Him to answer. God did warn me about Pat's death because of that nudge I felt after Pat said, "Next time you see me, I'll be looking fantastic." She was right, but not the way we both thought. I did not see her looking great months later, but I will see her looking great when I get to where she is. She's already looking fantastic. When I get to heaven, I will see her, and she will be looking fantastic!

He was teaching me that He did warn me, and He does warn us. We can often get so focused on what we are praying for that we miss the answer when it is different than what we are expecting. We reject that warning, as I did, for two reasons: We do not like the answer, thinking it is our own self-doubt talking. I did that. We also reject the answer sometimes because we have trouble with the concept that God knows something "bad" will happen and does not stop it.

God does talk to us in many different ways. In doing this, God is showing us that He is real, He is aware of this life crisis, and He is in the midst of the crisis. He will safely see His children through to the other side. That other side of our mess may not be what we think it should be, but if we are His children, through our faith in Jesus's atoning death on the cross and resurrection, we will win, whether here on Earth or in eternity.

No matter the pain or mess we are facing, when we don't get the answer we think we should have, we can still trust that God has a greater gain for us still to come. On the other side of the pain or mess, we will have learned a greater lesson we couldn't have even thought of. We will gain greater spiritual muscles to fight bigger battles later on. We will have greater peace, greater love, greater joy, greater hope, and greater faith having gone through greater battle or pain.

When I was a new Christian, I was made president of the ladies' ministry of the church I belonged to. To put it succinctly, the women of that church liked my leadership so much, they shortened my term from a year down to nine months. It caused me great pain. Because I was so enthusiastic for Jesus, I organized twice monthly meetings (once per month during the day for stay-at-home women and once per month in the evening for those who worked). I organized fund raising for mission projects, and God told me to start a biweekly prayer meeting. I probably "activity-ed" the ladies to a stress level off the charts. I felt personally rejected when they were really rejecting my activity level for the ladies of the church. It really hurt at the time. In hindsight, that painful period taught me how to love others. That, in the end, was a lesson way more valuable than all the pain I went through.

I encourage you to get in the fight and stay in the fight until the end. Don't give up. Hopefully, you will be encouraged to use the tools or weapons God has given us to equip us to defeat the enemy and to study further for yourself about these tools and others not listed in this book. By the way, the tools or weapons listed in this book are not necessarily in order of importance. They are in the order that God gave to me.

I also encourage you to continue to stand, having put on the armor of God and, having done all, to stand. Press through the darkness you are in, no matter how dark. Press through to victory or until God tells you to stop. Feel the love of Jesus that I try to convey throughout this book for you. It is His desire that you know you are loved beyond anything you can imagine. It is His desire that you know you are equipped by Him to do what He asks you to do. Jesus knew He had to go away after He paid the bride price for you (his blood and death). He redeemed you from the kingdom of darkness and carried you in His arms into His kingdom of light and love and truth. He gave us all good gifts so that we would lack nothing spiritually until we are united with Him for eternity. He made sure we, as His bride, have everything we need, which is much different than having everything we want. One is equipped. The other is spoiled.

To help you become better equipped, I have also included in the back of this book several appendixes of Scriptures. I accumulated these lists of Scriptures over years and used them to encourage myself and prayer groups with which I was involved. They are Scriptures from throughout the Bible. While we read the Bible regularly, sometimes it helps to gather together various Scriptures that address a particular subject. That list of Scriptures then shows us just how much God does say on a particular subject. I pray that these appendixes will encourage you and build up your faith as a soldier of Christ's so that you are a fearsome warrior for God.

You are His desire. Ask Him to reveal His love for you in these pages. You are so loved and so equipped, you can be a believer full of faith, hope, and joy because you know you have authority over every plan the enemy has to destroy you. It won't be always easy, but we can be strong enough as we stand in our faith, in His love, and with His armor on that the enemy quakes in fear of us. Welcome to boot camp, soldier!

2

The Belt of Truth

God gives us many wonderful names. We're called believers, sinners saved by grace, saints, children of God, sons and daughters of the king, little children, brothers and sisters of Christ, the bride, lambs, sheep, the redeemed. All these names depict pictures in our minds that should tell us a facet of who we truly are to our Savior and Lord. However, these are also all gentle names that give us a warm, fuzzy feeling of security. These names do not depict another aspect of our lives once we believe—the fact that we gain an active enemy who is out to destroy us in any way he can. Our enemy delights in destruction, and if he can't fully destroy us, he'll destroy what he can.

Like it or not, as soon as we decide Christ did indeed replace our sinful self on the cross we deserved but He did not, we are in a war. The truth is that we are in a war, whether we choose to believe it or not. So in addition to all the names listed above, we need to put "soldiers" and "warriors" on this list. Jesus warned us that the devil walks around roaring like a lion, seeking whom he can devour. The good news is that Jesus also gave us everything we need to overcome the enemy. As a soldier in the army of God, we are fully equipped for the battles we will face.

Jesus sent out seventy of his disciples in Luke 10:1–16. He instructed them in verse 9, "And heal the sick there, and say to them, 'The kingdom of God has come near to you.'" In Luke 10:17, the seventy returned, amazed that "even the demons are subject to us in

Your name." Jesus heard this joy-filled statement and then replied to his seventy with

> I saw Satan fall like lightning from heaven. Behold, I give you the authority to trample on serpents and scorpions, and over all the power of the enemy, and nothing shall by any means hurt you. Nevertheless do not rejoice in this, that the spirits are subject to you, but rather rejoice because your names are written in heaven. (Luke 10:18–20)

I think the scene in heaven looked like this: Jesus was standing next to God the Father when punishment was decreed on the rebellious angel Lucifer, also known as Satan. The banishment from heaven was decreed, and Satan fell from heaven. As Jesus watched him falling (current tense), he turned to the Father, asking for protection and provision for all of us against Satan. Jesus asked this of the Father before Satan even hit the ground of earth. Lightning travels so fast it is hard to measure its speed. Experiments have estimated that lightning travels through the atmosphere at anywhere between the speed of 2,500–93,000 miles per second. Within that time frame, Jesus got permission from Father to give us His authority over Satan here on earth.

Jesus says, "I give you authority to trample...over all the power of the enemy, and *nothing* shall by any means hurt you" (emphasis mine).

Notice the verb in "and *nothing* shall by any means hurt you." Jesus does not say nothing will harm us. The potential is indicated there, as in something *could* harm us, or *nothing* shall harm us. We have a part to play in this as a soldier. We have the opportunity to trample on all the plans of the enemy. The enemy knows this and knows the Word of God too. He is very smart, very powerful, and very cunning. He's just not original. He is not creative like our Father. He has tricks to deceive us, but his toolbox of weapons does have limits. Whether we win our battles or not is partially dependent upon us, or those praying for us, using the authority Jesus gave us.

In Ephesians 6, we are told to put on the armor of God.

> From now on, you must right away become strong in the Lord and in the power of His strength. You must continually be clothed with the full armor of God to enable you to stand against the strategies of the devil: because the wrestling for us is not with blood and flesh, but with the rulers, with the powers, with the world rulers of this darkness, with the spiritual forces of wickedness in the heavenlies. Because of this you must immediately take up the full armor of God, so that you would be able to resist in the evil day and when you have completely achieved all things, to stand. Therefore you should stand, after you have girded around your waist the belt of truth and have put on the breastplate of righteousness and have put sandals on your feet in preparation for the gospel of peace, in all things having taken up the long shield of faith, with which you have been enabled to extinguish all the burning arrows of the evil one: and you must immediately take up the helmet of salvation and the sword of the Spirit, which is the Word of God. (Eph. 6:10–17 ONM)

God specifically chose every word that is written in the Bible, and the order in which it is written. Why did He put the belt of truth first? When I think of putting on the armor, for years I said the prayer to put it on each day starting at the top of my head and just working my way down: helmet of salvation, breastplate of righteousness, belt of truth, feet shod with the preparation of the gospel of peace, shield of faith and sword of the Spirit. It was easier for me to remember it in that order, logical in my brain. Now I have trained myself to put the armor on in the order God lists it in Ephesians.

Many believe that the first piece of armor we put on is the helmet of salvation. But God did not list that first on the list. He starts the list for us with the belt of truth. Why?

The armor is a reference to a Roman soldier's outfit. The people of the time Ephesians was written would be very familiar with a Roman soldier's armor and have an immediate word picture in their minds. The belt that went around the waist of a Roman soldier was called a *cintus*. It had strips of leather hanging down in the front center. The number of strips indicated rank. The strips provided for ease of movement while serving as a barrier of protection for the lower abdominal area. The belt could also have been made out of metal. Whatever the material, the belt served primarily to protect the stomach and lower trunk area of the soldier.

This belt held the soldier's weapons. Each soldier carried a personal, smaller sword called a *pugio*, which was more like a dagger, with the blade about seven to nine inches long. This smaller sword or dagger was one of the weapons carried on the soldier's belt, usually carried in a sheath.

There was a second belt, a baldric, which went over one shoulder and held the scabbard for the soldier's longer sword. This would allow the sword to hang down the soldier's side without hindering arm movement—out of the way but accessible when needed.

The belt is a perfect image of a piece of armor that held the weapons of a soldier. I believe God listed the belt of truth first so we would be aware of the extent of weapons He provided for us to use in our battle against the enemy. God has given us Jesus's authority, which happened when Satan fell from heaven like lightning. He loves us so much that this was provided long before the cross. We have every weapon we need to complete the fight against the enemy.

Notice what is said in Ephesians 6:13b (ONM), "And when you have completely achieved all things, to stand." It doesn't say "if" you achieve all things. It says "when" you achieve all things. God is expecting us to achieve all things. "All" is an amazingly encompassing word. "All" covers everything we will encounter during our lifetime.

"All" covers even more than that. "All" covers everything anyone will encounter. This is why we are to pray for each other, lifting the needs of others up before the Throne in heaven, as well as our own needs.

Our victory over all the plans of the enemy for us, for our loved ones, our church, other believers, our city, our state, our country, the nations, unbelievers, and the world all starts with our armor. Notice that two times in the four verses of Ephesians 6:10–13, we are told to put on the full armor of God. We can't pick and choose which parts of the armor we want to wear on any particular day. We are to put the full armor on!

We can't say something like "I'm not an evangelist. I'm too shy." or, "I'm not knowledgeable enough to witness to anyone." We're told to "have put sandals on your feet in preparation for the gospel of peace" (Eph. 6:15 ONM). You may think you don't qualify for God's army, thinking something like "I don't even deserve to be in the kingdom of light. You don't know the horrible things I've done." No, I don't, but Jesus does, and He chose you anyway. None of us deserve to be in His kingdom. We don't deserve His love. He chose to pay the price for our sins, and He chose to convey or carry us from our life of darkness into the kingdom of His light. He says, "I've already dealt with your past. I want you to focus on your future." We belong to Him, and He loves each one of us so much, He joyfully endured the cross for our sake. He wants us to serve Him out of love too.

In John 14:12, Jesus assures us, "Most assuredly I say to you, he who believes in Me, the works that I do he will do also; and greater works than these he will do, because I go to My Father." Note that Jesus says we will do the works, not we might do the works. Furthermore, in John 15:14–16, Jesus says,

> You are My friends if you do whatever I command you. No longer do I call you servants, for a servant does not know what his master is doing; but I have called you friends, for all things that I heard from My Father I have made known to you. You did not choose Me, but I chose you and appointed you that you should go and bear

> fruit, and that your fruit should remain, that
> whatever you ask the Father in My name He may
> give you.

"Whatever" is pretty inclusive. Jesus reiterates this again in John 16:23b and 24b, "Most assuredly, I say to you, whatever you ask the Father in My name He will give you... Ask, and you will receive, that your joy may be full."

Jesus also promises to send us a Helper, the spirit of truth, also known as Holy Spirit. Furthermore, He promises that Holy Spirit will remain beside us and will be inside us (John 14:17). Holy Spirit teaches us all things, and brings to our remembrance all things that Jesus said (John 14:26). Again, "all" is pretty inclusive. When Holy Spirit brings it to our remembrance, that indicates we have to put forth an effort to put it in us, so He can remind us. We are to read the Word, listen to it, attend church, or do whatever it takes to get the Word inside us. We are to commit our thoughts each day to Holy Spirit, put on the helmet and armor, and quit fretting so much.

He gave us the armor to wear. It is called the armor of God. Each one of us is given a sword of the Spirit. Each one of us is given a shield of faith. Each one of us is given the full armor of God. We are to use these tools for ourselves and for others. When we do, we glorify God.

The Roman shield was a long shield that was tall enough that the soldier could hide behind it and be completely protected. It was made out of thick hardened leather that was able to extinguish a fire dart that the enemy fired at the soldier. It was also oiled in such a way that it could reflect sunlight back into the enemy's eyes, hindering the enemy's ability to see. This long shield could also have been made out of metal.

When necessary, the soldiers could stand in a circle with the shields lined up to form a solid wall around them. This is what we do when we pray for others. We unite our shields together to form a wall of defense around a hurting brother or sister in Christ. We fight because, like it or not, we are in a war. We joined the army of God when we accepted Jesus as our Savior. It is important we know all the weapons available to us, so we gain the victory and do not lose faith.

We are to be filled with a deep joy—the seventy disciples were joyful and amazed as they went about working the works Jesus told them to do. It is really fun and amazing to be used by God with the "right" word of knowledge, wisdom, or encouragement for someone. It is really fun and amazing to be used when God heals someone, when the person you just prayed with realizes the pain is gone and health is restored. There is much rejoicing and amazement there. It is appropriate and natural to rejoice and celebrate these victories. These emotions, though, tend to fade as time moves beyond those special moments of victory. In other words, our emotions peak and decline. Jesus does not want us to continually stay "pumped up" or "psyched" with our focus on some victory of the past. It is not realistic to stay this way. He does want us to mark and remember them, but life goes on.

What does bring a believer to a place of deep, abiding joy is the knowledge of the depth of love with which we are loved by our Savior and Father. We have been given every weapon we need to be victorious and every authority we need to appropriate as we walk our walk of faith. We were given these at the moment Jesus asked the Father's permission. We were *that* loved before Satan even landed on earth. That is amazing! That is why we are to rejoice—that we are *so* loved our names were written in the heavens before the serpent talked Adam and Eve into giving up the authority they had. Jesus had already received permission to give it back to us.

This is why we are to rejoice. This is why we can be a people who have faith, hope, and joy. We can be like little children dancing a joy jig. We are to be confident in God's love for us and not afraid of the dark things. We have the Light of the world to dispel the darkness.

3

First Weapon: Faith

The root of the word *faith* in Hebrew is actually a verb—an action. *Faith* means established, firmness (*Strong's* #529 and 530). The root for *faith* (*Strong's* #539) means "to build up a support; to foster as a parent or nurse, to render or be firm or faithful, to trust or believe, to be permanent." "Do you faith Jesus?" is a better translation of what we say in English, "Do you believe in Jesus?" Scripture tells us that without faith, we cannot please God. We need faith to even have a relationship with Him. Without faith, we have nothing. Habakkuk 2:4b says, "But the just shall live by his faith." The essence of faith is not just an intellectual belief. It is not just believing that God exists, or that Jesus was the Son of God and died for your sins. The concept of faith is faithfulness, the steadfast behavior that stems from the belief.

The first use of the Hebrew word for faith is in Exodus 17:11–12, regarding Moses's hands. As long as Moses's hands were upraised, the enemy was defeated. Aaron and Hur helped hold up Moses's hands as the battle against Amalek raged. "And so it was, when Moses held up his hand, that Israel prevailed; and when he let down his hand, Amalek prevailed. But Moses' hands became heavy; so… Aaron and Hur supported his hands, one on one side, and the other on the other side; and his hands were steady." The word *steady* is the same word as *faith* in Hebrew.

Faith is not super willpower. It is steadfastness. The believer lives by this determination, persists in God's ways, and is steadfast in obeying God, honoring God, being loyal to God. We are to have the actions and characteristics of faith detailed in Jude 20–23:

> But you, beloved, building yourselves up on your most holy faith, praying in the Holy Spirit, keep yourselves in the love of God, looking for the mercy of our Lord Jesus Christ unto eternal life. And on some have compassion, making a distinction, but others save with fear, pulling them out of the fire, hating even the garment defiled by the flesh.

Faith is a behavior, not just a belief and not just a theory. It is steadfast behavior, especially in specific tests and trials. Y'shua tells His disciples in Matthew 17:20, "For assuredly, I say to you, if you have faith as a mustard seed, you will say to this mountain, 'Move from here to there,' and it will move; and nothing will be impossible for you." Why did Y'shua pick the mustard seed? What is it like to have faith like a mustard seed? Mustard seeds are sown in early spring, and the dry seeds are harvested in early autumn. There are eight mustard seeds in each pod. There were eight people in Noah's ark. Noah had faith; he spent about seventy-five years building an ark 450 feet by 75 feet by 45 feet in a world where it had never rained. The flower of the mustard plant has four petals arranged in the shape of a cross. Faith without the cross is just plain hope. Faith through the cross of Jesus enables believers to do what God is telling us to do, regardless of how that looks in the natural world.

Mustard is easy and inexpensive to grow. From very small seedlings, mustard plants grow rapidly, between five and twelve feet tall depending on variety. Mustard seeds flourish on many different types of soils, tolerate extremes of weather without serious harm, and grow in such diverse places as Canada, the American Great Plains, Hungary, Great Britain, and even the Himalayas. Mustard is the largest spice by volume in world trade. The seed is only one-tenth inch in diameter. Faith is available to all, costs us little to obtain, should grow rapidly and flourish in many different types of hearts, and should be the largest output of the body of believers in Messiah.

The most interesting thing about having faith like a mustard seed is what is inside that seed. Mustard is 30–40 percent vegetable oil, a slightly smaller percentage of protein, and a strong enzyme called myrosin. The seed is odorless and tasteless when whole. When the mustard seed is chewed, or when mustard powder is mixed with water, it creates a chemical reaction between two of the constituents in the seed to produce an oil that was not present as such in the plant. That is what gives mustard its strong taste. When we mix our faith with His power, His Spirit produces great results that were not present before.

Jesus tells us in Luke 18:1–8 a parable about a widow seeking justice from an unrighteous judge. She refused to give up, and the judge eventually gave her the justice for which she was looking. Luke 18:1 says, "Then He spoke a parable to them, that men always ought to pray and not lose heart." In verses 7 and 8, Jesus explains that God is a righteous judge, not an unrighteous one like in the parable. "And shall God not avenge His own elect who cry out day and night to Him, though He bears long with them? I tell you that He will avenge them speedily. Nevertheless, when the Son of Man comes, will He really find faith on the earth?" If the unrighteous judge gave in to the continuous cry of the widow, how much more will our loving Father God do for us, if we continue to have faith in Him and His promises to us?

Jesus went about His ministry preaching that the kingdom of God was at hand (Right here! Right now!), healing the sick, confronting the wrong doctrines of the Pharisees, doing miracles, teaching the people, cleansing lepers, delivering people from wrong spirits, raising the dead, and so many other miracles according to John that there aren't enough books in the world to record them all. He warned his disciples not to rejoice in the victories. "Nevertheless do not rejoice in this, that the spirits are subject to you, but rather rejoice because your names are written in heaven."

We rejoice when God actually answers prayers. We give praise reports, which build up the faith of everyone who hears. It also releases faith into the atmosphere so that others can gain the victory too. A testimony about a miraculous healing, or provision, or breakthrough will often result in more of the same type of victory. Praise reports are important. Just as we high-five each other when we get on base in sports or score a touchdown in football, we celebrate when God does a miracle of any sort. If this is so natural for us to do, why does Jesus warn against this? He is not against celebration. Rather, He is stressing that this is just expected activity and outcome to Him and to Father.

Obedience to God, His Word, and His direction are expected behaviors for believers. Jesus gives an example of this in Luke 17:7–10. Jesus says,

> And which of you, having a servant plowing or tending sheep, will say to him when he has come in from the field, "Come at once and sit down to eat"? But will he not rather say to him, "Prepare something for my supper, and gird yourself and serve me till I have eaten and drunk, and afterward you will eat and drink"? Does he thank that servant because he did the things that were commanded him? I think not. So likewise you, when you have done all those things which you are commanded, say, "We are unprofitable servants. We have done what was our duty to do."

Jesus says we are servants. We are to do what our Lord and Master tells us to do. What is that?

Matthew 10:7–10 gives the answer: We are to go and do. "And as you go, preach, saying, 'The kingdom of heaven is at hand.' Heal the sick, cleanse the lepers, raise the dead, cast out demons. Freely you have received, freely give." In case we question what this means, Jesus adds in Matthew 28:18–20,

> All authority has been given to Me in heaven and on earth. Go therefore [note: not "if"

you go] and make disciples of all the nations, baptizing them in the name of the Father and of the Son and of the Holy Spirit, teaching them to observe all things that I have commanded you; and lo, I am with you always, even to the end of the age.

Mark adds in Mark 16:15–18,

Go into all the world and preach the gospel to every creature. He who believes and is baptized will be saved; but he who does not believe will be condemned. And these signs will follow those who believe: In My name they will cast out demons; they will speak with new tongues; they will take up serpents, and if they drink anything deadly, it will by no means hurt them; they will lay hands on the sick, and they will recover.

Jesus sent out seventy unnamed disciples in Luke 10. These were not the twelve apostles; these were just followers of Jesus. We have the same orders, the same anointing, the same benefits, and the same possibilities available to us today. God is no respecter of persons, which means He does not favor one person over another. While these orders may seem daunting and too difficult, Jesus would not have given them if they could not be accomplished. Our weapon to accomplish our "marching orders" of battle: faith. Jesus told us to do these things, so it is up to Him to anoint us to accomplish them. We all know not one of us can heal a fly or a mosquito; how can we heal another person? We don't even know if a fly or mosquito is sick, let alone have the ability to heal it. Not one of us can cleanse a leper, or raise a dead person. Jesus can. All we need to do is be willing to believe His words, obey His orders, and trust (faith) Him to work through us.

It is important that in the parable of Luke 17:7–10 that the Master says, "Serve me till I have eaten and drunk, and afterward you will eat and drink." At the Passover *seder* we commonly call the Last Supper, Jesus said, "For I say to you, I will no longer eat of it until it is fulfilled in the kingdom of God...for I say to you, I will not drink of the fruit of the vine until the kingdom of God comes" (Luke 22:16–18). That is why Jesus refused to suck on the sponge the centurion offered him at the crucifixion. The wine mixed with gall would have eased the excruciating pain Jesus was experiencing. Jesus keeps His word—He keeps His promises to us. He refused to drink the wine because He promised He would not drink until we are all together with Him at the marriage supper. At great personal pain to Himself, He kept His promise. He did not drink wine. He did this overlooked act of suffering specifically to prove that He is trustworthy, and we can put our faith in Him.

We are to serve and obey Jesus until He eats and drinks at our marriage supper. Then, we can eat and drink with Him. Until that time, we are to obey and do what He commands us to do. We are servants of Jesus and we are to do the works that Jesus did. He expects us to do so, and He expects results if we obey. The results are natural and fully expected, thus fully provided already by Jesus.

Jesus prayed in John 17 and said that He did not lose any one that He has called to follow Him wherever. He prayed to the Father so that we will overcome and have victory over every attack from the enemy. In John 17:12, Jesus says, "And none of them is lost." John 17:6 says, "And they have kept Your Word." John 17:10 says, "And I am glorified in them." John 17:19 says, "I sanctify Myself, that they also may be sanctified by the truth." Jesus said: not one was lost; they have kept God's laws. Jesus is glorified in the disciples; because Jesus is sanctified, the disciples are too. These things are stated as facts in His prayer. These things have already been completed and accomplished.

Jesus was talking about the disciples in this prayer, yet He was also praying for all of us. "I do not pray for these alone, but also for those who will believe in Me through their word; that they all may be one, as You, Father, are in Me, and I in You; that they also may be one in Us, that the world may believe that You sent Me" (verses 20–21). What had the disciples done? Jesus said they have kept God's Word.

Yet Scripture shows that many times over the three years that Jesus was living with them, they failed to "get it"—to understand what He was saying. They failed to comprehend the Word. They argued with the scribes. They argued among themselves. They vied for who was to sit next to Jesus in heaven. They failed to cast a demon out of a boy. They were afraid many times. Most of them stayed in the boat. Yet Jesus said they have kept God's Word. Jesus loves them, and He loves us.

After Jesus was resurrected, He told Mary Magdalene, "Go to My brethren and say to them, 'I am ascending to My Father and your Father and to My God and your God" (John 20:17). He was talking to disciples who had abandoned him, denied Him, left the tomb, and were in hiding, full of fear. He was reminding them (and us) of His prayer in John 17, before His arrest, where He said the Father is in Me and I am in the Father, and His disciples are in Them. He is saying that the disciples were not rejected now, they were not orphans, but that they are still one with Jesus. He still loves them and still expects them to do what He told them to do.

Here is an example of expectation from my life. My daughter had a boyfriend who was older than her in high school. He apparently skipped a lot of classes. I mean a lot. He just did not seem to care about school. I am also sure his parents did not know he was skipping school. He had so many detentions that he could not possibly fulfill them by sitting in detention after school before graduation. My daughter talked the teachers into accepting her offer to sit in detention on his behalf so he could complete the requirements and graduate on time. She spent her afternoons sitting there with him after school so that each day fulfilled two detentions.

She sat next to me at his graduation. As he walked by, she was crying and said, "I'm so proud of him!" It shocked and bothered me that she was so emotional and proud. I didn't say anything until I took the time to figure out exactly what was bothering me. I replied to her, "It is expected to graduate high school." In America, education through high school graduation is free if going to public school. This is not the case in most other countries. Elsewhere, students must pay to go to school, even elementary school, plus buy books and own a school uniform. Many students come from families too poor to pay these expenses, so schooling is limited. In America, a high school diploma, or GED equivalent for those who were unable to complete high school, is considered the bare minimum of education required for the job market. Simply put, it is expected that students graduate from high school. More specifically, in our family, it was not only expected that our children graduate high school, we expected them to graduate college too. What bothered me was that my daughter had lowered her expectations down to his level.

My son has a song by a Christian group that he listens to, which says in part, "Defeat is not an option." To a Christian, failure should not be an option. Defeat is not an option. If you've read to the end of the Bible, we win. The enemy is already defeated. He spends a lot of time telling you otherwise. His tactics include fear and discouragement so we lower our expectations from Jesus's standard down to the level at which the enemy wants us to function. When he gets us there, he can get us.

Many believers have gotten sidetracked into looking to the future for the kingdom. The thoughts are that we just somehow survive until we get there—to heaven—then things will be good. There is a total disconnect in their thinking between life here and life once we get to heaven. This has led to an emphasis by the western church on salvation in current times. Salvation is the first step in discipleship. Jesus did not say go and make people saved. He said to go and make disciples. That is much more than salvation. That's duplicating Jesus's behavior and thoughts in others.

The Pharisees at the time of Jesus were looking for the Messiah to come. They were actually looking for a leader, the king, the Son of David, who would free them from Roman rule and lead the nation of Israel again. They had somehow overlooked and forgotten the suffering servant portions of Scripture that would deal with the sin issues once and for all times. They were looking for someone who would lead a free Israel. The Pharisees had limited vision for the future whereas God had a much greater thing in mind—one sacrifice for all times and all people. God had a plan for a much bigger nation of followers than just the Israelites. He wants to graft many more branches into the vine already established in Israel. The Pharisees missed the Messiah standing right in front of them, face-to-face, because their expectations were limited to what had been in the past.

We have a powerful scripture in Ephesians 3:20: "Now to Him who is able to do exceedingly abundantly above all that we ask or think, according to the power that works in us." That's where our faith level should be! The faith meter hidden in this scripture is off the charts. The mercury in the thermometer of our faith should be so high that it blows through the top of the glass holding it in. If we can think it—whatever "it" is—if we can imagine "it," we are not thinking big enough. If we can ask "it," we are asking with limited vision of potential. That's amazing!

When we are asking for Him to move for His plans and His glory, we can expect to be astounded by the extent of victory we have. God has a plan and wants us to ask Him to help us accomplish each task for Him His way. God also wants to accomplish things in our own lives for our benefit. He wants to bless us. We have the promise here that God is able to do whatever for our benefit in ways that are beyond our ability to measure His ability. That same power, the authority Jesus asked Father God to give to us, works in us. We have it—it is a weapon of ours granted by God. Do we "faith" God enough to raise our expectations to His level? Do we dare to think God will help us get "exceedingly abundantly" beyond our circumstances?

The rest of the sentence is in the next verse, which also is very important. The entire sentence reads, "Now to Him who is able to do exceedingly abundantly above all that we ask or think, according to the power that works in us, to Him be glory in the church by Christ Jesus to all generations, forever and ever, Amen." This power is for our benefit but more importantly this power is for His glory. God is not a wish fairy, a Santa Claus that might give us everything on our wish list, or some other type of generous spirit we can manipulate. His power is for His glory. It is not for our glory. It is not some lightning bolt of power we just zap at someone when we are irritated. It is for us to glorify God the Father by Jesus to all generations.

Faith generates more faith as we give testimonies of things God has done. A woman in a Bible study I attended mentioned that her daughter was having premature labor. The baby would be extremely premature, and she requested prayer that the baby would stay in the womb at least two more weeks. Of course, we all said we would pray. I was able to share with her the story of what God had done for another friend of mine who also had a baby born extremely premature. That baby was born nine weeks early but had no complications. That little premature baby is now a teenager and playing football, baseball, and golf. I reminded the anxious soon-to-be grandmother that if God had done it for my friend, He could do it for her daughter too. As soon as I got with my husband, we prayed for the situation and protection on the possibly very premature baby. This premature baby girl was born twelve weeks early, but she was healthy. Upon doing the C-section, the doctors discovered that the umbilical cord had bunched up to the size of an adult fist with a clot forming. The premature birth saved this precious little girl's life. When things aren't going according to our plan, we need to have faith that God has His plan and it will prevail, to our benefit.

God often reminds us of a past situation when we are hearing about a current situation. Those reminders are to build our faith and to build the faith of the people in the current situation by hearing the testimony of what God did in a similar situation. We then know we can pray for God to work like He did in the past with the understanding that God brought that particular situation to our remembrance because He's about to do the same sort of work. Knowing God is faithful to us builds our faith to release the miraculous into our present.

Joshua is a good example of someone who remembered God's promises, fought to gain the victory, and walked in faith. In Joshua 5:13–14, the night before Joshua went into battle at Jericho, the Angel of the Lord appeared to him. Joshua asked, "Whose side are you on?" The angel answered in what appears to be a curious, weird way: "Neither" in the New King James Version. That answer would not be comforting to me as a leader about to take my people into a battle.

But look at the previous chapters in Joshua. Joshua 1:2b–3, 5 records that God told Joshua, "Arise...go...to the land which I am giving to…the children of Israel. Every place that the sole of your foot will tread upon I have given you, as I said… No man shall be able to stand before you all the days of your life… I shall not leave you nor forsake you." Joshua was specifically chosen by God to lead the people into the Promised Land because he was one of the few who chose to believe God's word when He told them to go in and take the land forty years before. Numbers 27:18–22 records this choice.

> And the LORD said to Moses: "Take Joshua the son of Nun with you, a man in whom is the Spirit, and lay your hand on him; set him before Eleazar the priest and before all the congregation, and inaugurate him in their sight. And you shall give some of your authority to him, that all the congregation of the children of Israel may be obedient… At his word they shall go out, and at his word they shall come in, he and all the children of Israel with him—all the congregation. So Moses did as the LORD commanded him. He took Joshua…and inaugurated him."

God reminded Joshua again through Moses in Deuteronomy 3:22 and 28, "You must not fear them [the inhabitants of the land], for the LORD your God Himself fights for you… But command Joshua, and encourage him and strengthen him; for he shall go over before this people, and he shall cause them to inherit the land which you will see."

Joshua was facing battle to take Jericho. It says in Joshua 6:1, "Now Jericho was securely shut up because of the children of Israel; none went out, and none came in." Jericho was a fortified city, with solid walls surrounding it. Joshua was about to receive unusual battle strategy, which he was then going to have to convince all of Israel to obey and follow. Part of that strategy was silence. Joshua had to convince about forty thousand men prepared for battle (Josh. 4:13) to not say a word but simply to march around Jericho. In order to implement this strategy and accomplish this great victory, Joshua had to know that this was the plan of God. God opened his eyes to see the Commander of the army of the LORD to solidify Joshua's faith, which he could then impart to his troops.

God loves us so much that He gives us His Word, His visions, His reminders to build up our faith. Faith is a weapon of warfare on our belt of truth. Faith is essential to winning any battle over the enemy. Faith is essential for relationship with God. Using our faith has the power to take down stronghold walls and gain victories over obstacles that seem impossible in the natural. This is one reason we can be people of joy. We have faith, and we have hope.

4

SECOND WEAPON: PEACE

One part of our armor is our shoes—our feet shod with the preparation of the gospel of peace. Preparation means just that—prepared, with provision, made ready. *Webster's Collegiate Dictionary* defines *preparation* as "the action or process of making something ready for use or service or of getting ready for some occasion, test, or duty." Further on, *Webster's* defines preparation as something that is prepared, like a medicinal substance made ready for use. When we put on the armor of God, hopefully daily, we put on our feet the preparation of the gospel of peace. We are thus already prepared to go out and tell others about God's plan of salvation through Y'shua. We do not need to go through great training or years of scholarly study to effectively tell others about Jesus. We are already made ready for use, with provision, to accomplish what Jesus told us to accomplish—to be witnesses, to testify, about what Y'shua has done for us.

Acts 1:2 says that Jesus gave orders to His disciples before He ascended into heaven: "The day in which He was taken up, after He...had given commandments to the apostles." Jesus didn't give suggestions. He gave orders. This means it is not optional for us to obey what He said. He expects us to do what He told us to do. We just have to trust in that provision—the making us ready that He does—and do it. Our feet are beautiful to Him—He gave us His gospel of peace to wear on our feet, to shod them so we could go everywhere and anywhere.

Isaiah 52:7 says, "How beautiful upon the mountains are the feet of him who brings good news, who proclaims peace, who brings glad tidings of good things, who proclaims salvation, who says to Zion, Your God reigns!" This verse is talking about Y'shua's feet. We often take this verse to mean the feet of any missionary who is going to tell others the gospel. Where was Y'shua standing when He gave His orders to the disciples in Acts 1? On the mountains. Acts 1:12 states, "Then they returned...from the mount called Olivet, which is near Jerusalem, a Sabbath's day's journey." Jerusalem is in a mountainous area. Jesus fulfilled this prophecy. He stood in the temple (located on top of Mt. Zion) declaring the gospel of peace. He walked down the mountains declaring the gospel of peace. He walked through the mountains declaring the gospel of peace as He went between the Galilee area and Jerusalem.

Isaiah 61:1–3 then says that this anointing Y'shua has is transferrable to all His followers:

> The Spirit of the LORD GOD is upon Me, because the LORD has anointed Me to preach good tidings to the poor; He has sent me to heal the broken-hearted, to proclaim liberty to the captives, and the opening of the prison to those who are bound; to proclaim the acceptable year of the LORD, and the day of vengeance of our God; to comfort all who mourn, to console those who mourn in Zion, to give to them beauty for ashes, the oil of joy for mourning, the garment of praise for the spirit of heaviness; that they may be called trees of righteousness, the planting of the LORD, that He may be glorified.

We are equipped to go tell others the Good News. When they hear and believe, they become trees of righteousness planted by the river of life (see Psalm 1) and God gets glorified in our obedience of telling. God gets glorified when someone believes the gospel and gets set free from evil and sin. God gets glorified when depression becomes joy, when sickness becomes health, when captivity becomes liberty, when the brokenhearted become *pray*-ers and *praise*-ers.

Nahum 1:15 says, "Behold, on the mountains the feet of him who brings good tidings, who proclaims peace! O Judah, keep your appointed feasts, perform your vows, for the wicked one shall no more pass through you. He is utterly cut off." We are to take any vow we make to God seriously because He has cut off the wicked one (Satan). God is worthy so we should honor Him by fulfilling any vows we make. We often make vows in ignorance and stupidity, but sometimes our vows are intentional. For example, as believers, we feel God calls us to fast certain things or for specific time periods. We decide to obey, and we need to fulfill that vow. One time, I remember God called me to fast meat for forty days. I did. On the last day, we were on our way to Sunday morning service. I was thinking about being able to enjoy a nonvegetarian meal in the immediate future, when God started talking to me about another forty-day fast. I said, "Okay, but what do You want me to fast now? I just got done fasting meat." He answered, "Bread." I shuddered! To give up bread (which to me also meant rice, pasta, and all other grains) for forty days! I didn't know if I could do it. Then I thought, *Wait a minute! How can you say no to God?!* So I said, "Okay" and started a second forty-day fast. That's one example of fulfilling vows.

Another example is what I did in foolishness before being baptized in Holy Spirit. Our third child, our youngest daughter, was a toddler at the time. We had a nanny who decided we should use all the camping equipment we owned but hadn't used. We booked a weekend at a beautiful campground by the St. Croix River that separates Minnesota from Wisconsin. A flash flood came through the campground the first night as the result of severe storms that swept through that area. Everything was muddy, including our one-hundred-pound dog. I was in the tent trying to clean out the mud. My husband put the dog in the back of our jeep to keep him out of the way and out of the mud. In doing so, he wrenched his back. Our youngest daughter sat in a folding lawn chair that was set up around the campfire.

As I watched from inside the tent, the chair slowly collapsed while she sat still on it, throwing her into the campfire hands first. She had third-degree burns on the inside part of her wrists, and blisters on her palms. She was treated and bandaged at the closest hospital (at least a half-hour drive from the campground). The emergency room doctor said the burns were severe enough that she would need to have skin grafts and surgery and would be severely scarred. While the initial healing was happening, the bandages would need to be changed, the burns cleaned, and medication reapplied daily.

Since our company retreat was scheduled immediately following this disastrous camping weekend, I was going to be driving two to three hours one way to our pediatrician for her care. One of our company's salesman and his wife offered to pray for our daughter for healing. I accepted. Our family was attending a church, but living life for ourselves. I knew of Jesus and had been water baptized around age twelve. I knew Jesus died because of my sins, and I also knew I deserved to go to hell for those same sins. I had no idea that God wanted to be actively involved in my life, or that He cared about what happened to me and my family. I took my daughter to have this couple pray for her before we left on our long drive back to our city for the first day's doctor appointment. They prayed for healing, and for her memories to be erased so she wouldn't fear fire but would know to keep safely away from it. As I listened to them pray, I silently made a vow with God in my head. If He would heal the burns so they were not third degree, if my daughter would not need surgery, I would tell the pediatrician about this prayer time and that God had answered the prayer.

A lot of people have made these types of vows—bargaining with God for what we want—making a vow as if God could be persuaded or motivated by our frail actions. In His mercy and grace to both my daughter and me, God did answer these prayers. The pediatrician took off the bandages and examined the burns. He looked at the emergency room records that had been sent over and said, "These are not third-degree burns. They are only second degree. She won't need surgery." He then told me he was going to be back soon to clean the wounds and rebandage them. He quickly popped out the door before I could say anything. I knew I had to tell the doctor about the prayer that our salesman and his wife prayed.

To my horror, a nurse came in instead of the doctor. I had vowed to God that I would tell the doctor. While I was mentally dealing with this shock and horror, she was efficiently working and done before I could pick my jaw up off the floor. I grabbed her by the arms as I silently asked God if telling a nurse would be acceptable to Him instead of the doctor. She got my testimony regarding that prayer full force. She looked at me strangely, but I think it was because I was acting in desperation to fulfill a vow to God. I knew enough to know you don't mess with God! I had such a grasp on her that she couldn't have escaped before I finished telling her about this couple's prayer and how God heard that prayer and changed the burns from third degree to second degree.

When we witness to someone about God's works, we utilize our feet being shod with the preparation of the gospel of peace. There is a weapon of peace that we have tucked on our belt of truth; however, that is a weapon of warfare. Let's examine this weapon a bit.

Luke 24:36–49 records Jesus appearing to His disciples after His resurrection and before His ascension into heaven. Jesus stood in the midst of the disciples, like he was suddenly visible to them. The first thing He said after becoming visible to them was "Peace to you." Peace means "Shalom" in Hebrew, which is much more than just a calm/quiet or lack of fighting or lack of fear. *Shalom* means overall well-being, including welfare, health, prosperity, safety, happiness, tranquility, sufficient provision for physical needs such as food, clothing, and housing, and rest. Shalom is "no good thing withheld" according to the glossary at the end of the One New Man Bible.

God has a covenant of peace—an irrevocable legally binding agreement to provide peace, Shalom, to those who follow and obey Him. He gave that covenant of peace to Phineas (see Numbers 25 for the complete story). God also promises His covenant of peace with the nation of Israel in Ezekiel 34:25–26:

> I will make a covenant of peace with them,
> and cause wild beasts to cease from the land; and

31

they will dwell safely in the wilderness and sleep in the woods. I will make them and the places all around My hill a blessing; and I will cause showers to come down in their season; there shall be showers of blessing.

The list of blessings goes on for the rest of that chapter. As believers in Messiah, we are grafted into the vine, according to Romans, which means these promises also include all believers in Jesus. Father God restates this covenantal promise in Ezekiel 37:26: "Moreover I will make a covenant of peace with them, and it shall be an everlasting covenant with them; I will establish them and multiply them, and I will set My sanctuary in their midst forevermore." While the temple will eventually be restored in Jerusalem (coming down from heaven), and Jesus will reign from an actual throne in an actual temple in Jerusalem, right now God has set His sanctuary within my heart (and the heart of every believer) when I gave it to Him. The indwelling of Holy Spirit is a current fulfillment of this promise to me, a grafted-in branch on the vine of Jesus.

This covenant of Shalom requires something of us too. Malachi 2 is a warning for the priests to listen and obey or be cursed. Verses 5–6 state,

My covenant was with him, one of life and peace, and I gave them to him that he might fear Me; so he feared Me and was reverent before My name. The law of truth was in his mouth, and injustice was not found on his lips. He walked with Me in peace and equity, and turned many away from iniquity.

The covenant of peace, or Shalom, requires the recipient (believer) to revere God and His name (Yehovah), to speak and teach truth at all times. This is God's truth, as laid out in the full scriptures, not man's theology of parts of the scriptures. We can't pick only the parts of Scripture we like to read. I knew a woman who only read the

New Testament. We need to read both the Old Testament and the New Testament. The New Testament should not stand alone since it is the recording of the life of Jesus on earth, a history of the believers after His ascension (Acts) and then clarifications of Old Testament scriptures in light of Jesus's revelations/teachings. Jesus didn't come to start a new religion. Jesus was Jewish, and His only scriptures were what we call the Old Testament, and what Jewish people today still consider the Word of God. Jesus only quoted from that Word. We should know it too.

Psalm 29:11 says, "The LORD will give strength to His people; the LORD will bless His people with peace." As I've said above, I am now His child, part of His people, which happened when I chose to accept Jesus's death as atonement for my sin. I chose to leave my sinful ways and start living according to His rules. All His rules are for my benefit. This is what is referred to in Psalm 85:8: "I will hear what God, the LORD will speak, for He will speak peace to His people and to His saints; but let them not turn back to folly." There's that requirement on our part again as recipients of the covenant of Shalom—we can't turn back to folly. We have to walk in the truth of His teaching, all of it. When Jesus appeared to His disciples in Luke 24, He fulfilled this prophetic verse in Psalms. He spoke Shalom to His people and to His saints. Jesus said "Peace to you" in Luke 24:36.

Psalm 119:165 also indicates the obedience required to receive the covenant of Shalom. "Great peace have those who love Your law: and nothing causes them to stumble." Only God is in the business of changing hearts. Man may try, as witnessed by all the self-help books over all the years, but God promises to change our hearts in Jeremiah 31 among other places. Only God can give us a love for His Teaching, His Torah, His Word. When I was a child, my grandfather would read the Bible every night. I adored him, and wanted to do the same. I think I got my first adult Bible when I was in fifth grade. I tried reading it, starting in Genesis and thinking I had to read it straight through like any other book. I got as far as the "begats" and quit. I don't remember now if I was reading about the generations of Adam in Genesis 5 or those of Noah in Genesis 10. I just remember that someone begat someone else, and I got lost. I felt like I had plodded through with great difficulty to that point. I just gave up. When I received the baptism of Holy Spirit with the evidence of speaking in tongues, I decided I should try to read His word again. I opened the Bible, started reading, and thought, *Wow! This is so easy to understand!* The difference was Holy Spirit was now inside me to help me. God had taken my heart of stone (selfish, self-centered, sinful) and replaced it with a heart to know God: "Then I will give them a heart to know Me, that I am the LORD; and they shall be My people and I will be their God, for they shall return to Me with their whole heart" (Jer. 24:7). God put His respectful awe in my heart so that I would not depart from Him (Jer. 32:40).

I did not even know these scriptures existed, but I had the experience of being able to read and understand His Word, which stood in stark contrast to my own feeble efforts so many years before. The reality and experience comparison were my proof that God was trustworthy, that He did indeed exist. He loves me, and He loves me enough to not leave me as I was when I came to Him. He was already beginning to change me to be more His child and less my own sinful self. That process is a life-long process. I just need to continue to keep my heart available to Him so He can keep changing it.

Jesus is so patient and gentle. When he popped into the group of disciples, Luke 24:37 says the disciples became terrified: "But they were terrified and frightened, and supposed they had seen a spirit." He started the conversation with "Peace to you," which should have reminded them of all the places in Scripture where God promises peace to His followers. We've touched on some of them here. The disciples would have had the Torah (Old Testament) memorized and been familiar enough with it to be able to instantly recall these various references of Shalom. However, fear is a powerful thing, and that's why the enemy uses it against us so effectively. The two disciples who had seen Jesus disappear in front of them (road to Emmaus experience, especially Luke 24:31) were in the midst of explaining all this to the rest of the disciples when Jesus suddenly appeared to the entire group.

The disciples were not just terrified and afraid—a redundant thought. They were terrified. They were also afraid they were seeing a spirit. In modern words, they were terrified, and they thought they were seeing a ghost. Sometimes the things God wants to do with us are far outside our normal thoughts. That's when the question "Do you *faith* God?" should pierce our hearts. The two disciples "found the eleven and those who were with them gathered together, saying, 'The Lord is risen indeed, and has appeared to Simon!' And they told about the things that had happened on the road, and how He was known to them in the breaking of bread" (Luke 24:33–35). As those two had their eyes opened to see Jesus, he became invisible for them (verse 31).

All those gathered together just heard that testimony, but now they were being swallowed by terror, fear, and doubt. Jesus's next words were "Why are you troubled? And why do doubts arise in your hearts?" (verse 38). Doubt and fear were rising like a tsunami over their hearts and minds. Fear and doubt go hand in hand. They are an unholy alliance that Satan uses to rob us of our faith, our trust in God.

In my own life, I experienced a long two years of inflammation of my bursa in my left hip. Every step was painful, although I could walk. Lying down was painful. The extreme pain made me tired fast, and I could not find any relief. I eventually got a shot of cortisone from my doctor. It didn't work as well as he thought it would, and he then informed me that bursa inflammation could go away on its own after a year or two. Not the news I wanted to hear! After at least a full year, maybe two, I was still seeking God for healing. Nothing the doctor or chiropractor did helped to ease the pain.

I asked a prophetic friend for advice while talking with her on the phone. She said that she felt God was going to heal me instantaneously. Faith leaped in my heart. It was such a strange feeling; there is no other way to describe it. I instantly became excited and knew that it was going to happen *now*. It was like a fire in my heart of hope and joy and faith. She then prayed for me. In that brief earthquake of time when faith leaped in my heart, I also allowed fear and doubt in. It was like evil forces were right there with arrows of fear and doubt poised to fire into my mind the instant faith rose up. Evil forces cannot read a person's thoughts. Only God is omniscient and can know your thoughts. But somehow, they fired the arrow of fear and doubt, which I allowed into my thoughts while my friend was praying for me. I started thinking that maybe the healing would take place at church the next morning, not over the phone right then. I started questioning whether God would indeed care to heal me at all since it had been so long that I had been living in pain. I started worrying that I was not "worthy enough" for God to heal me. I doubted that God would consider me "worth" healing. All these thoughts occurred within the few minutes she was praying.

Doubt is negative talk about God's character and/or your worth. The serpent in Genesis said to Eve, "Did God really say...?" (Gen. 3:1–5). He cast doubt in Eve's mind about what God said since he always misquotes God's words, saying God told them not to eat of every tree of the garden. Eve bought into that lie with the response that God told Adam and her not to eat or touch the one tree. She added to the rule God had given them. The serpent then smeared God's character further by indicating that God knew they would become like God if they did eat from that tree. Satan implied that God was trying to keep Adam and Eve from being like Him. Satan implied that God was insecure, petty, and craved all the power Himself and was not willing to share it. The serpent even contradicted God's warning that they would die by saying, "You will not surely die." The serpent did a thorough job of casting doubt about God's character and His love to Eve, and he robbed Adam and Eve of life, life in the Garden, and their dominion over the earth.

I allowed that doubt and fear to rob me too. After my friend finished praying, my hip felt so much better, and I did not wake up from the pain that night like I had every night for the past two years. However, I still had a remnant of the pain deep in my hip. I went up for prayer at the altar time at church for healing, thinking that maybe it would go away when they prayed, like I had been thinking while my friend prayed for me the night before. It didn't. God had wanted to heal me fully the night before, but I allowed doubt and fear to convince me that the healing would take place sometime later, maybe even at church.

I can tell you that I repented from allowing that unholy alliance of doubt and fear into my thoughts. In God's grace and mercy, He took most of the pain away. I had to live with the rest until the natural (and long) process of healing took place and the bursitis eventually went away in the hip. Fear and doubt are powerful tools in the hands of our enemy.

What can we do when fear and doubt overwhelm us? What I should have done while my friend was praying for me: fight back with truth and use that covenant of peace weapon hanging on our belt of truth. Truth in my situation was that God is my healer. I should have claimed scriptures regarding healing, such as where it says that Jesus went around healing all who came to Him (I know I qualify in "all"). I should have claimed scriptures that God loves me; Jesus paid the price in full for my salvation, therefore I am a child of God and no other work is necessary to qualify me for any blessing of my Father's. That's truth, and these types of verses line up with the covenant of peace that is mine.

In Luke 24, Jesus asked, "Why do doubts arise in your hearts?" The fact Jesus asked this indicates that doubts don't have to rise up in our hearts. When they do, we have the authority to push them back down and out—there is no room for doubt in a faith-filled heart that is at peace. Think of an argument with someone—it takes two people to argue. Have you ever tried to argue with someone who wouldn't argue with you? I have. When I was younger, my emotions would get out of whack about once a month. Most times, it was not a problem. I remember one time, though. I was very frustrated because I could not balance the checkbook. I was off a couple of cents and could not find the error. It frustrated me that my husband would write a check and not properly record the amount, or that he would use the cash card to withdraw money from the account and not write it in the checkbook. These things were frustrations, but really had nothing to do with the two cents I could not properly reconcile. Since my emotions were out of whack, I was looking for an argument to vent my frustrations. My husband just refused to engage in that. He ignored my verbal jabs and stabs. He just told me I was wonderful and would find the mistake. In essence, he answered my anger with love. That takes the fight out of another person and leaves no room for a fight. In staying in a place of love for me, my husband retained his peace.

No amount of ranting and raving on my part would move him from his place of peace. That's what the covenant of peace should do for us. No matter what the enemy is trying to shout in our ear, or heart, we can calmly tell him to get out of our way and out of our life.

Let me give you another example. My oldest daughter came home from college with Cocoa, a fifty-pound dog. She and I had talked on the phone while she was at college about her getting a dog. My husband had overheard only a portion of that conversation, and assumed I had encouraged her to get this dog. That was not true at all. My daughter also neglected to tell us several things, such as she rescued this dog from a friend, who had rescued it from someone else. This was now a one-year-old dog that had never been inside a house before. I would call that a pertinent fact. This dog was not housebroken, or trained in any way. We had Baker, a really large dog (around one hundred pounds) who was housebroken. Cocoa and Baker got along extremely well. They would play with each other, roll around, and bang into the screens on my windows. Soon every screen in the house had holes. What wasn't damaged by them playing was damaged because Cocoa wasn't trained and would jump up with her front paws on the screens to greet whatever excitement she saw out the window—people, squirrels, other dogs being walked down the street, etc. Soon I could not open any windows because of the damaged screens. Mosquitoes could swarm through the screens in formation and not have to break ranks to get through the holes.

In addition to the windows now being useless, my carpet was ruined. Cocoa was not housebroken. Baker, being the head dog, felt it necessary to mark any territory Cocoa had marked, which meant my carpet got double doses of dog "stuff." Baker forgot he was house trained and staked his claim to his house all over my upstairs and downstairs—wherever Cocoa had left her current "deposits" inside the house.

I tried to put Cocoa on a long chain in the yard in an attempt to save the few spots of carpet not stained by the dogs. She also liked to dig holes. My yard became full of holes that were two feet deep. It looked like a minefield after the mines were blown up. My husband was mad and blamed me. I was mad and yelling at my daughter about the dog. I was a stay-at-home mom at that time, and she had a job, so I was stuck with the dog all day long. It never occurred to me that the dog hadn't been trained at all. I thought the dog was having difficulty adjusting for some reason. Of course, nothing I tried worked because I was attempting to solve a different problem than what my real problem was.

As a student, my daughter didn't have any extra cash, and Cocoa didn't have the required shots a dog is supposed to have: rabies being most crucial, and a license by the city. I reminded her many times about the legal requirements for the rabies and license. She finally got frustrated with my nagging and said, "At least the dog's not foaming at the mouth!" The next day, she left the house for a long time, and Cocoa was in a crate in her room. I could hear the dog whining while cooking supper in the kitchen, but I refused to go let the dog out, trying to make the problem my daughter's and not take ownership myself. It began to pour rain (another summer severe storm) and my daughter came home about an hour or two later than I expected her. I told her to immediately go and let the dog out. She wanted to wait because of the rain, but I told her the dog had been whining for hours already and deserved to be taken outside to relieve herself. She came running back into the kitchen because Cocoa was foaming at the mouth. An emergency vet bill (expensive!) later, we were told that Cocoa had swallowed a toad. She did get her rabies shot that weekend, though.

Overall, I was having a bad summer. I was mad at my husband being mad at me, and I was having real trouble dealing with a destroyed house—all carpet and screens ruined. I finally had an argument with my husband, and told him just how mad I was about that dog. My daughter walked in unexpectedly and overheard what I said. To be honest, it would have been hard to not hear what I said. I expect the neighbors probably heard me too. I knew I had to go apologize to my daughter for my words. I told her I was sorry she heard me say them in that way, but that I was not sorry for the words. Cocoa was a problem!

We called our pastor, and he came over to counsel and pray with us. As he drove over, he prayed for guidance. All God told him was that I had given my peace away. It was a big lesson for me. I learned that since my peace is a gift from God, Satan has no right to take it away from me. He can, however, talk me out of it. I can choose to give up my peace. I had done that and was miserable all that summer. Satan had smoothly disarmed me of my weapon of peace. He was tormenting me, and I was allowing it. We prayed together, and I repented of giving up my peace and took it back from Satan. My heart was finally at peace again, and my husband and I talked with our daughter about the problem of Cocoa. She agreed to allow me to put an ad in the paper, and we gave Cocoa to a good home for her. She was a hunting-type dog, and the new owner was going to train her for hunting. It was good for Cocoa, my daughter no longer had a pet she couldn't afford, and I no longer had a loving but destructive force rolling through my house twenty-four hours a day. I learned a huge lesson about peace, and I can use that peace to fight back against Satan's plans to torment or harass me.

Jesus says, "Peace I leave with you, My peace I give to you: not as the world gives do I give to you. Let not your heart be troubled, neither let it be afraid" (John 14:27). This covenant of peace is a powerful weapon of warfare against Satan. A heart at peace, a spirit at peace, a soul at peace can see God's hand at work in a situation much more easily and clearly that one that is agitated, fearful, or doubtful. When we are fearful or doubtful, we focus on the problem, whatever it is that Satan is doing at the moment, rather than on the solution— our Father in heaven and His power to protect and keep us.

First Thessalonians 5:23–24 says, "Now may the God of Peace Himself sanctify you completely; and may your whole spirit, soul, and body be preserved blameless at the coming of our Lord Jesus Christ. He who calls you is faithful, who also will do it." When we have appropriated the peace that is ours by covenant, we are full of faith, hope, and joy.

5

THIRD WEAPON: JOY

The first mention of joy in the Bible is 1 Samuel 18:6: "Now…
when David was returning from the slaughter of the Philistine,…
the women had come out of all the cities of Israel, singing and danc-
ing,…with tambourines, with joy, and with musical instruments."
The Israelites had wanted a king because they were weary of going
to war against the various nations that attacked them continuously.
In the past, God would allow Israel to be attacked after they strayed
away from His ways. When the children of Israel cried out to God, He
then raised up a judge to lead them in a victory (the book of Judges
gives the details of these times). The Israelites eventually wanted a
king to be their leader since the surrounding nations had a king, and
part of any king's job was to lead his people into the battles. God gave
them Saul as their first king, and he did lead the battles for Israel.

It wasn't such a pretty picture, though: "Now all Israel heard…
that Israel had also become an abomination to the Philistines… Then
the Philistines gathered together to fight with Israel, thirty thousand
chariots and six thousand horsemen, and people as the sand which
is on the seashore in multitude" (1 Sam. 13:4–5). Saul had an army
of three thousand in total, no chariots, and no recorded horsemen
(1 Sam. 13:2). The people trembled as they followed Saul (1 Sam.
13:7). At first, Saul won the battles, despite the odds against them
because the Lord was with Saul. However, "There was fierce war with
the Philistines all the days of Saul" (1 Sam. 14:52).

The Philistines pulled out their secret weapon—a giant over nine feet tall named Goliath who taunted the Israelites for forty days. They were demoralized, fearful, and discouraged. The rules of engagement were that the loser would be servant of the victor. Israel probably expected Saul to fight Goliath since he was king and head and shoulders taller than his people. Forty days of taunts with silence in response from the Israelite camp was telling. No man in the Israeli army was confident enough or willing to go against Goliath in a one-to-one fight.

To illustrate just how fearful and demoralized the army was, they were willing to send a young shepherd to fight for them. Imagine the scene: the youngest brother of three of your fellow soldiers showed up with cheese, bread, and grain, and volunteered to fight Goliath. Saul heard of this, and after only one time of questioning David's ability, gave David his own armor to use (which David rejected). The entire army looked on as this young shepherd walked out onto the battlefield with his shepherd's staff, five stones, his sling, and a backpack on his back. Even though David had served as Saul's armor bearer and musician (1 Sam. 16:21–23), Saul turned to his army captain and asked who this young man was. Even the army captain didn't know (1 Sam. 17:55–58). An entire army and its king were willing to put their fate in the hands of an unknown shepherd boy. On the human level, that's desperation.

No wonder the women came out with joy upon David's return! He had single-handedly secured their liberation from the Philistines, their freedom, and smashed fear, discouragement, demoralization, and dismay all at the same time. The first definition of "joy" in *Webster's Dictionary* is "the emotion evoked by well-being, success, or good fortune or by the prospect of possessing what one desires."

All Israel was experiencing the emotion evoked by well-being, success, and the prospect of possessing what they desired—to live in peace.

In English versions of the Bible, the word *joy* appears 165 times in the KJV, 218 times in the NIV, 182 times in the NAS. We therefore know that God talks a lot about joy in His word. Joy is not the same as happiness, or optimistic cheer. Joy is a much deeper feeling.

Biblically, it is our response to possessing God's shalom (peace, over-all well-being, tranquility, justice, provision, health, etc.) for our life.

Nehemiah 8:10 says, "Do not sorrow, for the joy of the LORD is your strength." The primary root of the word *joy* in this verse means "to rejoice, make glad, be joined." Putting the definition into the verse, you can read it as "do not be grieved, for you are joined with the LORD and that is your strength." The LORD has the ultimate strength. He is the All-Powerful, All-Knowing, Ever-Present One Who promises to never leave you or forsake you. You and He are joined together. When Satan attacks you, He is attacking God. Remember that Scripture says we are the body of Christ. I may be a cell of an eyelash, and you may be a cell of His finger, but we are part of the body of Christ. If Satan attacks His eyelash or finger, he is attacking the body of Christ. We're joined together with Christ. That's amazing. That is cause for joy. As David sang, "What is man, that you are mindful of him?"

Joy is our strength because God is our strength. Joy is a weapon of warfare. In 1913, Eleanor H. Porter wrote a children's best-selling novel, *Pollyanna*. It was such a literary success that the word "Pollyanna" became the term for anyone who had the similar optimistic outlook and attitude as the main character in the book. It was made into two movies. Pollyanna's optimistic outlook always saw the good in every situation and every person and stemmed from her determination to find something to be glad about in every situation. Her optimism was contagious. Eventually, the townspeople where she went to live with her stern aunt after being orphaned changed their dour attitudes, and they began to see their glass as half full instead of half empty. Pollyanna's joy of life was contagious.

Jesus is God, and Jesus is outside time. Imagine that God is holding a gel capsule in the palm of His hand, like a Vitamin E liquid gel capsule, or a gel cap of a pain reliever of some type. One end of that pill is the beginning of time, and the other end is the end of time. Somewhere in the liquid inside that gel cap is where you are at this moment in time. That image is a picture of how big God is. He is the great I AM, who is with Abraham and Moses at the same time He is with you currently, and He is with all his children as end-time events unfold. He is so big, He is outside of time, but can totally surround that gel capsule of time that is tiny in His hand.

Jesus was there with you in your past. Actually, He is currently there in your past. Jesus is with you now. He promises to never leave you or forsake you. Jesus is also there ahead of you in your future. He'll be there with you when you get to your future, but He is also there right now, ahead of you. If you can understand that concept, then you can have joy and peace because you know that nothing takes God by surprise. When life throws you a curveball, or a giant disaster of some kind, God was there before you got into the mess. Taking this concept further, if you were terrified by something or someone as a child, Jesus was right next to you at that moment. Jesus was there when you were offended or hurt by someone in the past. Jesus was right there with you when it happened. If you didn't know Him then, it didn't matter. He knew that you would know Him and was with you.

Remember that Jesus paid the price for all our sins on the cross. That means He took the sin of the person who offended you. That offense against you was taken to the cross by Jesus. Hebrews 9:26, 28 says, "He has appeared to put away sin by the sacrifice of Himself...so Christ was offered once to bear the sins of many. To those who eagerly wait for Him He will appear a second time, apart from sin, for salvation." The person who offended you, if they repent and accept Jesus's death as atonement for their sins, is forgiven. That offense against you, committed by them, is forgiven. Jesus also took that offense for you on your behalf. When the person offended you, Jesus took that offense. He loves you so very much that He willingly took that offense and that hurt so that you would not have to bear it.

We have to be willing to give that offense to Jesus. We can't carry that hurt, bitterness, or offense around in ourselves. It is toxic to our soul and body and robs us of our joy. Forgiving that person does not mean you give them a free pass on what they did. You do not give them permission to do what they did. It does mean that you recognize that Jesus took that offense and hurt on your behalf, and you acknowledge that Jesus has it. You release that person into God's judgment regarding that offense and hurt. You also release that hurt in your heart to Jesus, Who has carried it for you. Forgiveness does not alter the facts of what happened. It does, however, nullify the pain. God takes the pain caused by those facts away. It no longer hurts. The facts are just that: facts. Forgiveness shatters the stronghold that offense/hurt has on your heart and soul and releases the joy of God instead of the hurt of man in your heart. The hammer of joy crushes the stronghold of bitterness or unforgiveness in your heart.

Y'shua prayed to Father God in John 17, before His arrest and death. He said in verse 13, "These things I speak in the world, that they may have My joy fulfilled in themselves." Jesus has given us the full measure of His joy. He has given us the completeness of His joy. What does that mean? He took all the offense and hurt (sins of others) plus all our sin, to the cross. Hebrews 12:2 says, "Looking unto Jesus, the author and finisher of our faith, who for the joy that was set before Him endured the cross, despising the shame, and has sat down at the right hand of the throne of God." Jesus endured the cross for the joy that was set before Him. He took our sin, our hurts, our offenses both given and received, and received the full measure of joy, which He then gives to us. We can live in a place of deep, abiding calm well-being: joy.

Let me give you a different perspective of this same concept. God gave me a vision in April 2007. I had read Mark 15, which records Pilate's sentence of scourging and crucifixion for Jesus. The soldiers then beat Jesus, spat on Him, and mocked Him. He was beaten beyond recognition, which was prophesied in Isaiah 52:14, "So His visage was marred more than any man, and His form more than the sons of men." After reading Mark 15, I sat and pondered all the beatings Y'shua endured. He had been beaten at the high priest's house, at the (illegal) nighttime trial after His arrest in the Garden of Gethsemane. He suffered from a lack of sleep. He was scourged. An entire band of Roman soldiers beat Him after the scourging. They put a purple robe on His bloodied shoulders and back, and a crown of thorns on His head. They beat Him with a reed about His head, spat on Him, and mocked Him. I saw a vision in my mind of Jesus as He was being scourged. I was in the crowd looking on. I started to weep because my sin put Him there, and because of the horror He was going through. He looked straight at me and said, "No! Don't cry! I'm doing this because I love you!"

I remember how his mouth looked—bloodied, with teeth sticking out in different directions, being knocked by the punches of the soldiers. His lips were swollen and bloody. His cheeks were bloody because His beard had been pulled out. The crown of thorns was on His head, and blood ran down His face from that. His eyes, though, were dark and passionate as He looked straight at me with the intensity of His love. He was giving me a gift and enduring these beatings because He loved me. It was a gift of love.

I then started thinking about how my husband and children give me gifts. My husband brought me coffee in bed every morning as a way of telling me he loved me. My children would sometimes make breakfast and bring it to me in bed. I would receive crayon pictures, valentine cards under my pillow from my children, or a present of some type for my birthday or Mother's Day. How strange they would have thought me if I had responded to these gifts and actions with tears, bemoaning how miserable a person I was, and that I did not deserve these love tokens. That actually would not be an appropriate response. They expect me to take the gift, the coffee each morning, and say thanks with a smile. They were offering me their love. Love offerings are not supposed to be rejected. How crushed my children would have been if I had refused to open the card or eat the breakfast they brought me, crying and saying how undeserving I was to even have such a gift.

Hebrews 12:2–3 says, "Looking unto Jesus, the author and finisher of our faith, who for the joy that was set before Him endured the cross, despising the shame, and has sat down at the right hand of the throne of God. For consider Him who endured such hostility from sinners against Himself, lest you become weary and discouraged in your souls." Jesus endured the cross because of the fullness of joy that He would receive on the other side. It is joy to give a gift to someone you love. It is joy to love someone. We are His joy. Conquering sin, giving us freedom and eternal life, are His joy too. Receiving that freedom, eternal life, His love, and relationship with Him are our joy. Being joined with God is our joy and His joy.

Further on Hebrews 12:18–25a says,

> For you have not come to the mountain that may be touched and that burned with fire, and to blackness and darkness and tempest, and the sound of a trumpet and the voice of words, so that those who heard it begged that the word should not be spoken to them anymore. (For they could not endure what was commanded: "And if so much as a beast touches the mountain, it shall be stoned or shot with an arrow." And so terrifying was the sight that Moses said, "I am exceedingly afraid and trembling.") But you have come to Mount Zion and to the city of the living God, the heavenly Jerusalem, to an innumerable company of angels, to the general assembly and the church of the firstborn who are registered in heaven, to God the Judge of all, to the spirits of just men made perfect, to Jesus the Mediator of the new covenant, and to the blood of sprinkling that speaks better things than that of Abel. See that you do not refuse Him who speaks.

God, without atonement for our sinful nature, is exceedingly fearful. Jesus offered Himself as the lamb sacrifice to pay the penalty for our sins. He did this for each one of us because He loves each one of us. It was joy for Him to do so, and He wants us to joy in this gift too.

Philippians 3:1 commands us to rejoice in the Lord. This means continually rejoice, to walk and live and abide in the joy. This is a safeguard for us. It is a weapon of warfare against the enemy. The enemy cannot shake someone who is grounded in this joy. No matter what happens, what the enemy does to this person, their trust, faith, love, and joy in the Lord keep their focus on Jesus and not on the enemy.

Just in case you think this applies to those who you think are good, but not you, consider Psalm 16:3, "As for the saints who are on the earth, 'They are the excellent ones, in whom is all my delight.'" When you accept Jesus's atonement for your sin and decide to live life God's way rather than your own sinful ways, you are a saint. Nowhere in Scripture does it call someone who believes in Y'shua a sinner after they made that decision. We are always referred to as saints. You are a holy one. You are an excellent one. You are the delight of God. You are not a partial delight, but you are all of God's delight.

Second Peter 2:7 says that God rescued righteous Lot. What was Lot like? In Genesis, Lot was selfish. He chose the best land for himself when Abraham gave him the choice of which way to go because they were too big to continue being together. Lot was self-focused. He offered his own daughters to sexually out-of-control men who were determined to satisfy their lusts to the point of almost taking down Lot's door. Lot was covetous. Lot wanted fame and power, probably like he saw Abraham had. He sat at the gate and therefore was a judge for Sodom. However, the people he judged did not respect him. Lot's affections for God were being destroyed by the ungodly atmosphere continually around him. Yet 2 Peter says God called Lot righteous. If God can rescue Lot and call him righteous, He can rescue us too and does call us righteous. Furthermore, God can rescue our loved ones who are also living in ways and atmospheres designed to destroy their affections for God and for their families.

Look at Y'shua's prayer in John 17:6. He says, "I have manifested Your name to the men whom You have given Me out of the world. They were Yours, You gave them to Me, and they have kept Your Word." Y'shua used past tense there—they (disciples and followers, which now includes us) have kept God's Word. We have not failed Him. We...have...kept... His Word. He goes on to say,

> They have known...they have received and
> have known surely...and they have believed...
> they are Yours...and I am glorified in them...
> Sanctify them by Your truth. Your Word is
> truth... I do not pray for these alone, but also

for those who will believe in Me through their word…that the love with which You loved Me may be in them, and I in them. (Verses 7–26)

The disciples didn't instantly understand everything Jesus told them, especially pre-resurrection like in John 17. Jesus still said they kept God's Word. Even after the resurrection, they were scared, doubtful, and unbelieving. Luke 24:38–41 says,

> And He said to them, "Why are you troubled? And why do doubts arise in your hearts? Behold My hands and My feet, that it is I Myself. Handle Me and see, for a spirit does not have flesh and bones as you see I have"… But while they still did not believe for joy, and marveled, He said to them, "Have you any food here?"

Jesus marveled at the disciples' reactions. I can picture Him smiling at the joy His friends were experiencing because they were with Him, touching Him. I can picture them touching Him, then putting their hands over their own mouths in astonishment, eyes open wide in surprise, laughter and amazement coming out. I can picture them falling into each other's arms, and falling into His arms, hugging Him because they are so excited and in love with Him.

Jesus marveled and ate to prove He's real, not a ghost. Jesus, in patience and love, did something else (besides popping in on them) to prove to them He's real. He is so patient with us, so in love with each one of us, that He will take the time to show us what He is trying to teach us in different ways so we "get it." He took the time to walk with two disciples on the road to Emmaus, explaining the prophecies regarding Messiah so that they understood. "Did not our heart burn within us while He talked with us on the road, and while He opened the Scriptures to us?" (Luke 24:32).

The disciples still had doubts. Peter decided to just give up and go fishing, and some of the others went with him. They were human just like us and didn't understand parts of what Jesus was saying or doing. Yet Jesus still turned over the running of His Church to them. He says, in essence, "I've trained you to act like Me, and I want you to go and make more people like Me." Jesus knows our failings and still loves us. Jesus says, "Go ahead! You can do this!" Romans 8:29–30 says, "For whom He foreknew, He also predestined to be conformed to the image of His Son, that He might be the firstborn among many brethren. Moreover whom He predestined, these He also called; whom He called, these He also justified; and whom He justified, these He also glorified."

Father God appointed us, called us, made us righteous, and glorified us. These are all past tense. These are already done in the Spirit. We just need to realize it. This is the joy of the Lord—we are joined with Him by His love. How great is that love? Paul prays for believers in Ephesians 3:17b–19: "That you, being rooted and grounded in love, may be able to comprehend with all the saints what is the width and length and depth and height—to know the love of Christ which passes knowledge." Psalm 103 extolls just some of what that love does for us. The extent of His love for us is revealed in the benefits of the Lord. God

- forgives all our iniquities;
- heals all our diseases;
- redeems our lives from destruction;
- crowns us with loving kindness and compassion (if we wear it, we should operate in it!);
- satisfies our mouth with good things;
- renews our youth like the eagle's;
- does acts of righteousness for all who are oppressed;
- does acts of justice for all who are oppressed;
- makes His way known to us, His children.

Ephesians 1:17–2:10 continues a portion of this list of benefits. God

- gives us His Spirit of Wisdom and Revelation (Holy Spirit);
- gives us the riches of His glory;

- gives us His inheritance which exceeds the greatness of His power in us.

The list is throughout scripture. Look for the benefits. Receive the gifts. Receive the benefits. Act on them. Walk in them. Abide in the joy of the Lord! He loves you! Be filled with faith, hope, and joy!

6

Fourth Weapon: The Word

The armor of God starts with us being told to put on the belt of truth. Jesus prayed that Father God would make us holy by means of the truth in John 17:16. The Word (the Bible) is truth. God cannot lie. He is so powerful that every word He speaks *is*: He spoke and the world was created. He speaks, and something is that was not before. Every word He speaks creates something. Psalm 33:6 and 9 says, "By the word of the LORD the heavens were made, and all the host of them by the breath of His mouth… For He spoke and it was done; He commanded, and it stood fast." The belt of the armor of God is made of His truth. The belt is the Word of God, the Scriptures.

A lie is a deception, an untruth, or the opposite of the truth. The devil is a liar. He deceives us and tries to tell us the opposite of what is really true. The next time the devil whispers a lie in your mind or some discouraging thought, laugh at him and speak the opposite of that lie out loud. For example, the enemy may be telling you that you are worthless and can't do anything right. The truth is that you can do all things through Christ Jesus Who strengthens you. The truth is you are very valuable to Him.

Jesus tells us how valuable we are to Him when He taught about the kingdom of the heavens in the parables of Matthew 13:44–47:

> Again, the kingdom of heaven is like trea-
> sure hidden in a field, which a man found and

hid; and for joy over it he goes and sells all that he has and buys that field. Again, the kingdom of heaven is like a merchant seeking beautiful pearls, who, when he had found one pearl of great price, went and sold all that he had and bought it. Again, the kingdom of heaven is like a dragnet that was cast into the sea and gathered some of every kind.

We are that treasure hidden in the field. Our hearts are treasures to Him. A treasure box is a container that holds treasure. We are containers that hold the Spirit of the Lord. We hold His Word inside us, adding more every time we hear or read Scripture. We are also the field. Adam was created from the dust of the earth. We are dust. Jesus was man, being born of Mary, but He was divine, having been born of a virgin. The man, Jesus, sold all that he had to buy the field and hidden treasure. Jesus paid it all—His life through His blood—to purchase us, the hidden treasure buried in the field of all humanity. Isaiah 13:12 is a prophetic word describing Jesus: "I will make a mortal more rare than fine gold, a man more than the golden wedge of Ophir." Jesus was, and is, the only One. There is no other. There is no other way to the Father. There is no other ever born of a virgin. There is no other sacrifice suitable for our redemption. Jesus is the mortal who is more rare than fine gold.

We are that one very precious pearl. We usually think the kingdom of heaven is the pearl or the treasure for which we have to sell everything in order to obtain it. While we do need to consider our old way of life, and our lives in Christ, as nothing, we also can look at these parables as describing how precious we are to Jesus. Jesus paid the price for our salvation. He willingly died on the cross. He did so for the joy set before Him, according to Hebrews 12:2. The man in the parable sells everything to buy the field "out of his joy." "He has delivered us from the power of darkness and conveyed us into the kingdom of the Son of His love" (Col. 1:13). I love the way the Scripture says it: Jesus conveyed us from the kingdom of darkness into the kingdom of light. He carried us in His arms into His kingdom. What a picture!

Jesus did not have to purchase the Earth, so we know that Jesus was not buying the Earth back from Satan. "The earth is the LORD's, and all its fullness, the world and those who dwell therein," declares Psalm 24:1. This was written after the fall of man in Genesis but well before Jesus's death and resurrection. Jesus did get the keys of death and Hades, but these two things were Satan's dominion. Man was given dominion over the Earth in Genesis 1:28: "Then God blessed them, and God said to them, 'Be fruitful and multiply; fill the earth and subdue it; have dominion over the fish of the sea, over the birds of the air, and over every living thing that moves on the earth.'" Satan talked Adam and Eve into agreeing with him instead of obeying and trusting God's instructions to them. Through that agreement, he was enabled to kill, steal, and destroy. Remember, death only came when Adam and Eve ate the forbidden fruit. Satan questioned God's character, His intent, His love for Adam and Eve and planted doubts in their minds about God's motives regarding God's command. They agreed with that slander when they bit into the fruit in disobedience. They gave their dominion over the Earth away. Satan's "rule" only happens through agreement with man. Satan was kicked out of heaven. Jesus watched him fall like lightning. However, God did not give the Earth to Satan to have dominion over it. Adam and Eve lost it to Satan through disobedience.

Jesus came "to seek and to save that which was lost" according to Luke 19:10. Mankind was lost, understanding of God's Word was lost, and man's dominion over the Earth was lost. Jesus spent his ministry years teaching the truth of God's Word, clarifying where man had misunderstood or added extra observations, burdens, or rituals onto the Word. He demonstrated God's power and authority by deliverance from evil spirits, overcoming the last enemy—death, and doing so many miracles that could not even be recorded due to quantity. Jesus rescued what Adam and Eve had given away: "All authority has been given to Me in heaven and on earth" (Matt. 28:18). Revelation 1:18 adds that Jesus took the keys of death and Hades from Satan.

In Matthew 16:19, Jesus tells Peter, representing all believers, "And I will give you the keys of the kingdom of heaven, and whatever you bind on earth will be bound in heaven, and whatever you loose on earth will be loosed in heaven." How do we bind and loose? With words. We bind when we forbid or do not permit something. We loose when we do permit something. We have the judicial authority given to us by Jesus to permit or not permit something, especially in the spiritual realm of the enemy. The judge first makes the decision verbally, then locks the prisoner up with the keys he has.

Jesus also gave us authority over the enemy's powers in Luke 10:19: "Behold, I give you the authority to trample on serpents and scorpions, and over all the power of the enemy, and nothing shall by any means hurt you." The serpents and scorpions are the demonic forces that work for Satan. We have authority over all the power of the enemy. "All" is a really inclusive word. Satan has no power that we do not have a greater power with which to overcome him.

The keys that Jesus gave us were costly to Him. He paid with His life to get them for us. They are costly keys for us to use. We have to walk in obedience and right relationship with God to use them. We can't "pick the locks" and fake our authority. Satan recognizes that fake authority and doesn't listen to those faking it. He doesn't have to. Only those with proper authority to use the keys are the ones Satan has to obey because they represent King Jesus as His ambassador and carry the full judicial authority to use the keys. The most costly thing to do with the keys is to not use them at all. Think of the parable of the talents in Matthew 25:14–30. The servant who merely buried his master's talent and then gave it back to him was declared evil and lazy by the master. We need to utilize the keys and to share the gospel with the unsaved to obtain their freedom from the kingdom of darkness.

We have to follow the model Jesus lays out for us in Matthew 16:19 when using the keys given to us. Remember it is whatever is permitted or in existence in heaven, or whatever is not permitted or not in existence in heaven. That is our model. We know that God's will is that none should perish but that all should come to repentance, according to 2 Peter 3:9.

Sometimes we make the mistake of praying for a miracle of healing for someone so that the doctors and nurses would believe in Jesus. However, that is not in Scripture. Jesus is the Word, according to John 1:1 and 1:14: "In the beginning was the Word, and the Word was with God, and the Word was God... And the Word became flesh and dwelt among us, and we beheld His glory, the glory as of the only begotten of the Father, full of grace and truth." When Jesus commanded someone to be healed, they were having a direct encounter with the Word of God.

We can command healing (notice Jesus never asked the Father to heal someone) but the gospel should be preached too. It doesn't have to be a full hour sermon, but truth should be spoken. The person being prayed for is having an encounter with the Living Word. If they are already a believer, it can be as simple as reminding them of what God's Word says about healing, such as "Jesus healed all who came to Him" or that the first Name of God that He revealed in Scripture is Jehovah Rapha, the God who heals. If they are not a believer, they need to be told that Jesus loves them. They need to hear the gospel so they can have the faith to receive the miracle of their healing. "So then faith comes by hearing, and hearing by the word of God" (Rom. 10:17).

Since God's Word is so powerful that it creates, God allows our words to also be very powerful. James 1:19 exhorts all believers: "So then, my beloved brethren, let every man be swift to hear, slow to speak, slow to wrath." It is often said we have two ears and one tongue for a reason. Listen well and watch what you say. James 3:1–9 talks about the tongue.

> If anyone does not stumble in word, he is a perfect man, able also to bridle the whole body... See how great a forest a little fire kindles! And the tongue is a fire, a world of iniquity. The tongue is so set among our members that it defiles the whole body, and sets on fire the course of nature; and it is set on fire by hell...but no man can tame the tongue. It is an unruly evil, full of deadly poi-

son. With it we bless our God and Father, and with it we curse men, who have been made in the similitude of God.

We can bless or we can curse with our tongue. The choice is ours.

We can sit around, talking about our problems with anyone who will listen, grumbling and complaining about the awful things that have happened to us or are happening in whatever mess we are currently in. We can talk about how bad that person is who did wrong to us, who made us mad or who hurt us. When we spend time doing this type of activity, we are empowering the enemy. When hurt or angry, our flesh wants to be justified for the feelings we are experiencing and maybe also for the revenge we are contemplating. However, the justification will not make us feel any better. We need to take that hurt to God and allow Him to heal it by choosing to forgive the person who hurt us. James says that no man can tame the tongue. But God can! We just have to come into agreement with Him.

When we speak God's Word over the situation instead, we release God's power into that situation. Y'shua's teaching before His arrest in John 14 talks about Holy Spirit as the spirit of truth:

> If you love Me, keep My commandments. And I will pray the Father, and He will give you another Helper, that He may abide with you forever—the Spirit of truth, whom the world cannot receive, because it neither sees Him nor knows Him; but you know Him, for He dwells with you and will be in you. I will not leave you orphans; I will come to you. (John 14:15–18)

The spirit of truth is next to us and also inside of us. The spirit of truth remains beside you and inside you.

The spirit of truth is the third Person of the Trinity, Holy Spirit, and we can simply ask Him into our hearts with a prayer asking to receive the baptism of Holy Spirit. The evidence to know we have received Holy Spirit is speaking in tongues, which sounds very strange to anyone new to tongues. The first thing I noticed after prayer to receive this baptism was that I was able to understand the Scriptures when I read them. We have looked at Luke 24 where Y'shua suddenly appears to the disciples after his resurrection, asking for something to eat to prove to them He is alive and real, not a ghost.

What was His purpose in all the activity recorded in Luke 24:36–49? Verse 45 says, "And He opened their understanding, that they might comprehend the Scriptures." It is like He lifted off the top of their heads and just poured understanding and revelation of the Scriptures into their minds. This is promised in Proverbs 2:6–8: "For the LORD gives wisdom; from His mouth come knowledge and understanding; He stores up sound wisdom for the upright; He is a shield to those who walk uprightly; He guards the paths of justice, and preserves the way of His saints."

According to Scripture, the purpose of Holy Spirit is to be our comforter, advocate, encourager, teacher, counselor, helper, to give us the power and the ability to follow "the way." We have the power to walk the walk of Jesus. It is not the destination. It is the power to live a lifestyle, not a map and route to take to heaven. Thomas asked, "Lord, we do not know where You are going, and how can we know the way?" (John 14:5). Thomas was asking for a map, a route to go where Jesus was going. Jesus answered and said, "I am the way, the truth, and the life. No one comes to the Father except through Me." On the surface, this answer looks like a route or map. But Jesus is talking about a lifestyle, walking the walk of Jesus. The spirit of truth is the third aspect of God revealed to us. Father, Son, and Holy Spirit are three aspects of the One True God.

Jesus is the way. Genesis 18:19 records God's thoughts about Abraham: "For I have known him, in order that he may command his children and his household after him, that they keep the way of the LORD, to do righteousness and justice." Abraham would keep the Way of the LORD. He had a veiled understanding of Jesus since he told Isaac, "My son, God will provide for Himself the lamb for a burnt offering" (Gen. 22:8) when he was being tested by God to offer Isaac as a sacrifice to God. He understood that Jesus was the perfect lamb sacrifice. Abraham didn't say "a lamb" but he said that God would provide for Himself the lamb. Not just any lamb would do. The Lamb was the only One Who would be acceptable.

Jesus is truth since He is the Word. Jesus is the life. We are His body; He is the head. We have our life in Him, and we have eternal life through Him. God made a covenant with the house of Israel in Jeremiah 31:33 of which we are also partakers since we are grafted into the root of Jesse: "But this is the covenant that I will make with the house of Israel after those days, says the LORD: I will put My law in their minds, and write it on their hearts; and I will be their God, and they shall be My people." Holy Spirit and Jesus are in us and beside us. The discourse and prayer in John 14–17 says that Jesus is in the Father, the Father is in Him, and we are in Him, and He is in us. The spirit of truth will be beside us and inside us. We have the life of Jesus in us, and we gain understanding of the Word by our teacher Holy Spirit. This is confirmed in Ezekiel 36:26–27:

> I will give you a new heart and put a new spirit within you; I will take the heart of stone out of your flesh and give you a heart of flesh. I will put My Spirit within you and cause you to walk in My statutes, and you will keep My judgments and do them…you shall be My people, and I will be your God.

That was why it was easy for me to understand the written Word after I had the spirit of truth living inside me, as well as being alongside me. The baptism of Holy Spirit, the spirit of truth, is a double blessing.

Y'shua then told the disciples that He was sending the baptism of Holy Spirit to them in Luke 24:49: "Behold, I send the Promise of My Father upon you; but tarry in the city of Jerusalem until you are endued with power from on high." Acts 1:5 differentiates this baptism from the baptism of water that John did. The baptism of Holy Spirit is recorded in Acts 2:1–12, which was also prophesied in Joel 2:28–29.

The purpose of the spirit of truth is to give us power. Many people think God gives us this power so we can overcome sin. Y'shua paid the price for sin at the cross. The sin issue was dealt with already. Holy Spirit gives us the power to resist temptation, the power to put our flesh under subject to the Spirit, and the power to walk in righteousness. Holy Spirit also gives us the power to enlarge the kingdom of God on Earth by instructing us as we go through each day. Hebrews 4:12 states, "For the word of God is living and powerful, and sharper than any two-edged sword, piercing even to the division of soul and spirit, and of joints and marrow, and is a discerner of the thoughts and intents of the heart."

The Word of God is alive. Jesus is alive, and He is the Word of God. The Spirit convicts us of our thoughts, corrects our understanding, and helps us live according to God's standard. Second Peter 1:3–4 also says this:

> As His divine power has given to us all things that pertain to life and godliness, through the knowledge of Him who called us by glory and virtue, by which have been given to us exceedingly great and precious promises, that through these you may be partakers of the divine nature, having escaped the corruption that is in the world through lust.

The baptism of Holy Spirit was God's promise and gift, which Jesus Himself promised to send to us. This is what enables us to become sharers of the divine nature, escaping our sinful lusts. John 15:3 says, "You are already clean because of the word which I have spoken to you." We are pruned, or cleaned, by the Word. As we read and study and listen to the written Word of God, God cleans and prunes us. Hard, dead branches need to be cut off, not pruned. We are connected to the vine, and branches need to be pruned to be more fruitful.

The spirit of truth also gives us the power to witness to others. Acts 1:8 says, "But you shall receive power when the Holy Spirit has come upon you; and you shall be witnesses to Me in Jerusalem, and in all Judea and Samaria, and to the end of the earth." This is Jesus telling His followers what the power is for—to be His witnesses.

In Acts 2:11, all the Jews at the temple to celebrate Shavuot (Pentecost) said of the disciples, "We hear them speaking in our own tongues the wonderful works of God." Peter stood up with the eleven disciples. The other eleven had been standing and preaching, speaking the greatness of God in various languages. It wasn't just Peter preaching, it was all twelve of them. Peter's sermon is the one that is recorded. We all have testimonies of the greatness of God. When we tell others our testimonies, these are seeds that are planted for a crop, a harvest of believers. Some are harvested right away, others later.

For a season, our family was running a business in Oregon. The office was below an apartment where we lived in summers. Things were very crowded and served multiple purposes. The washer and dryer for the apartment was also the washer and dryer for the business needs. They were located in a hallway where several desks were crammed along the other wall. It was tricky negotiating in the middle space to put laundry into the machines, take it out, and not bump the workers at the desks. We had some young adults working for us, and one young man was having his girlfriend come out to visit him. He had been sleeping on the living room couch in our apartment. He asked permission to have his girlfriend sleep with him. I told him that was not allowed, and explained why our family's faith in God could not allow this while under our roof. We had several discussions about it, and ultimately, he decided to move into a partially remodeled recreational vehicle for the time she would be visiting.

Our youngest daughter asked me why I told him no regarding his girlfriend sleeping with him. She asked this while I was trying to do laundry. I answered her, explaining that what he and his girlfriend really would be doing was a sin in God's eyes if done before marriage. I told her I could not control what he did on his own, but I could not give him permission to sin while sleeping in our living room. We had authority since it was our apartment, and he could choose to sleep there with his girlfriend sleeping elsewhere, or he could choose to sleep with her elsewhere.

What I didn't know until later was that another young woman overheard our conversation since she was one of the office workers crammed against the wall of the hallway at her desk. We didn't know her history, but she had broken her back in an accident and had been paralyzed. Her brother and his wife took care of her while she was paralyzed, loving her and gently witnessing to her daily since they were believers in Christ. She rejected at the time what they said, but the seeds had been planted. God eventually healed her broken back and she could walk. My answer to my toddler-age daughter brought all her brother's words back to her mind.

That night, she went to a church service in town and gave her heart to Jesus. Her brother had planted seeds, and I unknowingly added water so that Jesus could take her in His arms that night. She told me all this the next time I saw her. There is power in our words, even when we don't think anyone is listening.

The power of the Word is great enough to change a hard heart into a heart willing to receive Jesus. It is great enough to change any situation. Let's look at Matthew 14:13–33 where Jesus fed over five thousand people, then walked on water. Jesus had compassion on the enormous crowd and healed their sick ones. As evening came, the disciples wanted to send the crowd away so they could buy food for themselves. This is where Jesus's answer became interesting: "But Jesus said to them, 'They do not need to go away. You give them something to eat.'" The disciples recognized a problem that over five thousand people (there were five thousand men, but this did not count women and children) had. They brought the problem to Jesus, and He ordered them to solve it. They must have looked at Him in amazement and perplexity. They were thinking naturally, and Jesus was trying to get them to think supernaturally. They replied to Him, "We have here only five loaves and two fish."

Jesus took over and had the loaves and fish brought to him:

"Then He commanded the multitudes to sit down on the grass. And He took the five loaves and the two fish, and looking up to heaven, He blessed and broke and gave the loaves to the disciples; and the disciples gave to the multitudes. So they all ate and were filled, and they took up twelve baskets full of the fragments that remained." The five loaves of bread and two fish fed well over five thousand people, with twelve baskets of leftovers. God doesn't add; He multiplies!

There is a story in 2 Kings 4:42–44 of multiplying food too. There was a famine in the land, and Elisha was at Gilgal with the school of prophets. The pot of stew made for the prophets was accidentally poisoned with some type of gourds that were added. Elisha added flour to the pot and the poison disappeared. After that, a man came to visit Elisha and brought with him twenty loaves of bread and some newly ripened grain. Note that these were carried in the man's knapsack, which means these weren't large quantities of food. Elisha told the man to give these first fruits offering to the prophets so they can eat: "But his servant said, 'What? Shall I set this before one hundred men?' He said again, 'Give it to the people, that they may eat; for thus says the LORD: "They shall eat and have some left over"'" (2 Kings 4:43). He obeyed, they all ate, and they did have some left over.

What is the common thread in these stories? The word of the Lord: "For thus says the LORD." Many assume Jesus just thanked God for the food, like he was saying grace over it when it says He blessed it. I think it was something more along the lines of praising God for being the God who multiplies and cares about His people so much that He willingly does miracles of multiplication when needed.

After feeding the huge crowd, Jesus sent everyone away and sent the disciples into a boat while he intended to be alone to pray. The boat was being battered by wind. "Now in the fourth watch of the night Jesus went to them, walking on the sea" (Matt. 14:25). The disciples were afraid, thinking they saw a ghost. Peter got out of the boat and walked on water:

> And when Peter had come down out of the boat, he walked on the water to go to Jesus. But when he saw that the wind was boisterous, he was afraid; and beginning to sink he cried out, saying, "Lord, save me!" And immediately Jesus stretched out His hand and caught him, and said to him,

'O you of little faith, why did you doubt?" (Matt. 14:31)

God is love, and God never changes. That means that Jesus always treats us with love and respect. He will never humiliate, embarrass, or punish us for what we did not understand correctly or just did not understand. Yet Jesus calls Peter one of little faith. He was the only one who even got out of the boat! What does that make the other disciples? He wasn't talking to them, but to the only one who did get out of the boat being tossed around. When wind is on water, there are waves. It doesn't say how long Peter was walking on water. It could have been for only a few seconds, a few minutes, or half an hour or more. Why would Jesus call Peter one of little faith? It cannot be a derogatory comment because God is love, and love would never do that.

What Y'shua was saying had to be truth. Peter's faith was small in comparison to what Y'shua had been demonstrating they could accomplish in the last twenty-four hours. Y'shua showed them, when they couldn't think beyond five loaves and two fish, that God has given man dominion over the natural and they can operate in the supernatural. Twelve baskets of leftovers from that bit of food was supernatural multiplication. He then walked on water, and Peter did too. This should have increased Peter's faith because he was operating in the supernatural over the natural too. Instead, Peter allowed fear and doubt to overcome him. He began to sink from the supernatural into the natural. Peter was closer than the other disciples to under-standing what Jesus was trying to teach them because he was willing to get out of the boat. Jesus wanted all the disciples to understand that they were not restricted by the natural. Jesus wanted their faith to grow bigger, not stay little.

The Word of God is supernatural. It is alive. It is sharper than any two-edged sword. When we speak God's Word into any situation we are in, we are operating in the supernatural and taking dominion over the natural. Some people pray to angels for help. Some people order angels to action, but Scripture says in Psalm 103:20, "Bless the LORD, you His angels, who excel in strength, who do His word, heeding the voice of His word." Angels obey the voice of His word. When we speak the Word into a situation, angels obey the voice of that word since it is His word. Angels respond when we speak God's truth over our facts with "It is written..." or "God says..."

This is a very powerful weapon we have, and Satan knows it. He can quote scripture too, but he craftily leaves out some portion when he does use it. When he uses this tool to deceive people, it often leads to a spirit of religion where scriptures are taken out of context and the performance of acting/behaving/dressing a certain way becomes more important than the love behind every verse of Scripture. We need to know the fullness of the Scriptures, both Old and New Testament, and read around any specific verse to get an understanding of context too.

Satan's other way of disarming us of this tool is to send the unholy alliance of doubt and fear. If he can get us to doubt the power of truth over the natural, we won't use it.

Use the Word of God. Jesus used it against the enemy when Satan tempted him—"It is written..." The facts may say something bad, hopeless, fearful, terrible, or horrible, but the fullness of Scripture is life: supernatural life. Jesus tells us how to pray in Matthew 6:9–13, commonly called the Lord's Prayer. Look at verses 9–10: "Our Father in heaven, hallowed be Your name. Your kingdom come, Your will be done on earth as it is in heaven." We are calling on the Name of the Lord and we are praying His will when we pray the Scriptures since they are His Words to us.

Some battles require longer prayer times than others. As I write this, I have been praying about one specific situation for fifteen years now. I keep praying because I have promises from God that I will receive the answer I am praying for. I ran out of new words to say years ago! I had already prayed myself through the entire Bible, putting the name of the person I am praying for into the Scriptures and praying the Scriptures as Holy Spirit directed me. After that, a kind pastor recommended I use a praise and worship Bible, which I did. It had words to hymns and songs along the borders of the pages, and I even prayed them. I have been given visions about the situation, which I pray. I call those visions into being, into the here and now. I have been led by Holy Spirit to particular Scriptures, which confirm those visions, and I continue to pray them. I will do all the warfare I know to do, as directed by Holy Spirit, and I will continue to stand, having done all. I trust God's word, and He promises me this prayer will be answered. I just don't know when.

Two saints I knew were in ministry their whole lives. Retired from active, full-time ministry, they continued to do ministry in their old age. They told me about a time they went to a funeral, knowing that an acquaintance of theirs had died. They looked up the details regarding the funeral in the local paper and went. As they came to the casket, their first thought was "Wow! She sure changed." They then realized they were at the wrong funeral. Two women died at the same time with the same name, but this was a different woman than their acquaintance. The other thing they noticed was a young man weeping deeply by the casket. They went over to him to offer comfort and talk. He told them this was his mother and that she had prayed for many years for his salvation. He had been living life for himself, with no interest in God. Her death made him realize his own need for the God his mother knew. He was sobbing, thinking she would never know that he wanted her prayers for him to be answered and not knowing how to do it. They asked if they could lead him in a prayer for salvation. After that prayer, they assured him that his mother did know that God answered her prayers. The son left with peace in his heart. Some prayers take more time to be answered than others.

Some answers to our prayers will be answers we don't want, but God is sovereign. Just because God doesn't answer one prayer my way doesn't mean I can quit praying. I cannot build my theology upon my experiences. I can only build my theology upon the Word of God.

Take the weapon of warfare, the Word, and speak to your problem, your real estate, your checkbook, your wayward family members, your body, or whatever your problem is, as Holy Spirit directs you. Watch as your problems respond to the authority of the Word. Keep praying until you see the results or until God directs you otherwise. Keep your heart and mind open for God to speak to you about the situation. You may receive further revelation, more understanding, or different orders in the process.

Think of it this way: view the Word of God as a walkie-talkie on your belt of truth. You unclip it, put it up to your mouth and say, "Alpha and Omega, this is Beta team member. We have a situation here. I'm about to speak truth into this situation. Have the angels get ready since they respond to Your Word. I'm going to speak Your Word. You promise in Your Word that Your Word will accomplish what You send it out for. So I'm sending it out into this situation."

Isaiah 55:10–11 says,

> For as the rain comes down, and the snow from heaven, and do not return there, but water the earth, and make it bring forth and bud, that it may give seed to the sower and bread to the eater, so shall My word be that goes forth from My mouth; it shall not return to Me void, but it shall accomplish what I please, and it shall prosper in the thing for which I sent it.

When we realize the power of His Word and the authority He gives us to use this power, we can be full of faith, hope, and joy. When we realize the power in our own words, we can build others up, proclaim truth (even if you need to consider what you are saying as prophetic since it does not line up with current facts) into situations and encourage others rather than allow our tongue to tear others down. By watching our own tongues and using the Word, we can help others to become people of faith, hope, and joy too.

7

FIFTH WEAPON: POSITION IN AUTHORITY

"However, when He, the Spirit of truth, has come, He will guide you into all truth; for He will not speak on His own authority, but whatever He hears He will speak; and He will tell you things to come" (John 16:13).

The spirit of truth does not speak on His own authority. Holy Spirit is one third of the triune God of Abraham, Isaac, and Jacob—the God of Israel. Yet both Holy Spirit and Jesus do not speak on Their own authority. Jesus says in John 5:19, "The Son can do nothing of Himself, but what He sees the Father do; for whatever He does, the Son also does in like manner." He further says in verse 30, "I can of Myself do nothing. As I hear, I judge; and My judgment is righteous, because I do not seek My own will but the will of the Father who sent me." Jesus is under the authority of Father God. Jesus tells us in John 16:13 that spirit of truth hears what Father God says, and spirit of truth speaks Father God's words to us. Holy Spirit is under the authority of Father God too.

Being properly under authority is a problem for humans. God gave us free will when He created us. He came in "the cool of the day" to talk face-to-face with Adam and Eve. He created a beautiful place for them to live, with everything they would need. All the animals of the world were around them, and apparently Adam and Eve could talk with them. It does not record that Eve was surprised the serpent said anything to her, so it must have been common. If it wasn't common, Eve would probably have been too astonished to respond to the serpent rather than just have a conversation with it. God's only command to Adam was to not eat of the fruit of the tree of knowledge of good and evil (note that Adam was given the command in Genesis 2:16–17, and Eve was created in Genesis 2:22). God gave Adam and Eve free will, so they could choose to obey God instead of being some sort of robot that could only obey. God did so because He wanted a relationship with them. Love requires that freewill choice because love is a mental decision even more than it is an emotion.

Love is a conscious decision to be unselfishly loyal and act out of benevolent concern for the good of another. When I married my husband, I actually didn't know him well enough to honestly say I loved him. I saw his character—his honesty, his integrity, his willingness to work hard, his generosity, his commitment to keep his word, and many other wonderful characteristics. I was greatly attracted to those character traits of my husband. After I married him, I got to know him intimately. What I mean by this is that I knew every nuance of his moods, thoughts, and emotions as I lived with him. I fall more and more in love with my husband every day of my life because I know him better each and every day of life that we spend together. I ask him a lot what he's thinking or to talk to me because I care to know his very thoughts. This is actually a visual picture of our relationship with God.

When we make the decision to accept what Y'shua did on the cross for us, acknowledging our need for a savior from our sinful nature, we don't know everything about Him. Yet we choose to trust Him because of the love He extends to us—His unselfish loyalty and benevolent concern for our good. We trust the little bit that we see or feel and grow to know Him better every day of our lives. We can spend eternity looking at Him, seeing something new with every glance, and fall more in love with Him every day because of all the wonderful aspects of Him that we see.

Adam and Eve disobeyed. They rebelled. When they did, they stepped out from under the authority of God. When the serpent lied to them, he impugned God's character. Satan implied God lied to them, and even that God did not want Adam and Eve to be like Him in Genesis 3:4–5: "Then the serpent said to the woman, 'You will not surely die. For God knows that in the day you eat of it your eyes will be opened, and you will be like God.'" When Adam and Eve ate the fruit of the tree of the knowledge of good and evil, they were agreeing with the serpent's implication that God had ulterior motives of superiority over them.

Before I go further into how our position in authority is a weapon, I want to address Satan's lie to Eve. In John 16:7–11, Jesus says,

> Nevertheless, I tell you the truth. It is to your advantage that I go away; for if I do not go away, the Helper will not come to you; but if I depart, I will send Him to you. And when He has come, He will convict the world of sin, and of righteousness, and of judgment: of sin, because they do not believe in Me; of righteousness, because I go to My Father and you see Me no more; of judgment, because the ruler of this world is judged.

It is true all believers are better off (to our advantage) because Jesus did go away: He died and rose from the grave, conquering death and paying for all our sins with his sacrificial death. We are also better off because we now have a Helper, spirit of truth, Who can dwell inside us and alongside us, to teach, comfort, guide, and help us. What is part of Holy Spirit's role in the world? Jesus says it is to convict the world of sin, righteousness, and judgment. What does He mean? Holy Spirit convicts the world of sin. I was working as vice-president of a financial planning firm. Part of my job was to hire and fire employees. I occasionally submitted some portions of bills from my personal credit cards to the company because they were business expenses that I charged on my personal credit card. I had hired an accounting clerk, and I had a problem every time I took a bill to him for payment.

I felt convicted and sinful every time I was around this man. I found myself explaining every time why I wanted him to pay the bill

I was submitting, like I needed his approval. I would get so frustrated with myself. I hired him. I had authority to sign the company checks as vice president. We were audited every year, so my submissions for reimbursement had to be legitimate or the yearly audit would have questioned the reimbursement. I couldn't understand why I felt such a need for his approval.

After I received the baptism of Holy Spirit on my first trip to Israel, I realized why I was having issues in my head and heart with this accounting clerk. He never did anything that was out of line as an employee. He was a great employee and a great accounting clerk, although probably underemployed at the time since he had lots of talent and skill. The issue wasn't him; it was somehow me. I realized he had Holy Spirit; he had a close personal relationship with the God I barely knew before that trip to Israel. I just knew it almost immediately after my own experience with Holy Spirit. What I felt coming from him was Holy Spirit's conviction of my sin. Just the presence of God in our lives can convict others of their sin and need for a savior.

Holy Spirit also convicts the world of righteousness. Righteousness is defined in *Strong's Concordance* as equity, specifically of character or act, justification. We are justified, or made righteous, by our faith in Y'shua. He said, "Because I go to My Father and you see Me no more." We cannot see Him, yet we believe in Him, we "faith" Him. We live and act based on that belief. Let me give you a visual image. As I was praying one morning, I saw a great heron fly into the rushes at the edge of a lake below where I was. He was hard to see in the rushes, yet I saw the heron go in there and knew that the bird was there. He stood so still, and blended into the rushes so well that he became almost invisible. Yet his reflection in the still water of the lake was perfect. It was very clear. We can't see Jesus, but we know He is here, just like I knew that heron was there. We are called to be the reflection of Jesus here on Earth. We are to be so like Him in love and in character that the world looks at us and sees Jesus. Jesus is not here in a physical body right now so the world can look at Him and see Him. We are called to righteousness, and with Holy Spirit's help, we can be the reflection of Jesus that the world does see.

Here is another illustration of this same concept. Light refracts, and we see a rainbow of light in the refraction. However, when we look directly at a crystal glass or vase, or whatever is refracting light, we do not see the refraction. Similarly, we do not see the rainbow refraction when we look at the bevels on a mirror or window. Only in the reflection do we see the refraction. We have beveled glass in a panel by our front door. When the afternoon light hits it, the rainbow is not seen in the glass. The rainbows appear all the way down my stairwell as the light refracts through the beveled glass and reflects against my wall. In the morning, the sun reflects off some crystal glass I have in the living room, and I can see rainbows of color around the room. The crystal itself does not show the colors, but the reflections do. Again, we are called to be the reflection of Jesus here on Earth. We can't see Jesus, but we know He is here. We are to be so like Him in love and character that the world sees Jesus as they look at us. They see the various colors of the light of Jesus since we are all individuals and made differently. We make up the rainbow of light that is Y'shua.

Holy Spirit points out our sin, and Holy Spirit points out our righteousness. We have equity of character with God when we allow Him to take over our heart. We are not equal to God; He is holy, which means there is no one and nothing else like Him. But He looks at us through the blood of Jesus and doesn't see our sin; He sees us as clean, pure, without sin. That's what having equity of character means. It is just as if I'd never sinned: justification. God is clearly superior to all things, all creatures, all humans. He doesn't have to have hidden ulterior motives of superiority. He is superior. He is love, and He desires us to have a relationship with Him. He is so powerful that He can vaporize all His creation in one thought, but He doesn't. He delights to hear us talk to him.

Paul says in Romans 1:16–17, "For I am not ashamed of the gospel of Christ, for it is the power of God to salvation for everyone who believes, for the Jew first and also for the Greek. For in it the righteousness of God is revealed from faith to faith; as it is written, 'The just shall live by faith.'"

In Romans 3:22–24, Paul says, "Even the righteousness of God, through faith in Jesus Christ, to all and on all who believe. For there is no difference; for all have sinned and fall short of the glory of God, being justified freely by His grace through the redemption that is in Christ Jesus."

Finally, Holy Spirit convicts the world of judgment. Satan has not just been defeated; Satan has been judged. Satan has been condemned to damnation under divine law. Holy Spirit reminds us of that, so we as believers can walk in the victory and power that Y'shua has given to us. This brings us back to authority. Holy Spirit does not speak on His own authority. Jesus prayed in the garden, "Not My will, but Yours, be done" (Luke 22:42). He also taught us to pray to Father God: "Your will be done on earth as it is in heaven" (Luke 11:2). It is not our will, but God's, that matters. It was God's will that Adam and Eve not have knowledge of evil. He wanted them to remain pure and innocent, only knowing good by knowing God. Adam and Eve freely chose their own will over God's will. They stepped out from under God's authority. The consequences of that choice are still unfolding many centuries later.

Proper positioning in authority is very important to God. Satan knows this. It's one of the three things he tempted Jesus with. Satan even used the same tactic with Jesus as he did with Adam and Eve: questioning the integrity, intent, and character of God and trying to plant doubt. With Adam and Eve, he said, "Did God *really* say...?" With Jesus, he said, "*If* you are the Son of God..." Jesus knew who He was. Satan knew who He was too. Thankfully for us, Jesus never wavered in His character, integrity, or intent.

Matthew 4:5–6 records the temptation where Satan took Jesus and placed Him on top of the highest point of the temple in Jerusalem. "Then the devil took Him up into the holy city, set Him on the pinnacle of the temple, and said to Him, 'If You are the Son of God, throw Yourself down. For it is written: 'He shall give His angels charge over you,' and, 'In their hands they shall bear you up, lest you dash your foot against a stone.'" The devil is quoting from Psalm 91 in this temptation. It is interesting to look at all of Psalm 91. We always need to look at context of Scripture as well as content, especially when being quoted by the enemy of our souls. Psalm 91 starts out with, "He who dwells in the secret place of the Most High shall abide under the shadow of the Almighty." Dwelling in the secret place of the Most High means being under His authority—it's His dwelling place. He's the authority there. "Abide under the shadow of the Almighty" also means being *under* His authority. Psalm 91:2 is a declaration that "the Lord, 'He is my refuge and my fortress, my God, in Him will I trust.'" Again, this is talking about authority: refuge, fortress, trust. All these are benefits—places of safety—for believers, with God over us (in authority).

What did Satan want Jesus to do? He wanted Him to jump off the top of the temple. Satan actually did a prophetic act when he placed Him on the pinnacle of the temple. He put Jesus on top of the temple. Jesus is the head; we are the body. What is the body of Christ? The entirety of believers, commonly called the church—that is what was represented by the temple in Jerusalem. It is where all believers were to come and worship God. Satan wanted Jesus to turn that relationship upside down in this temptation. He wanted Jesus to fall, or jump, or throw Himself down so that the temple was above Him and He was below. What Satan wanted Jesus to do was put the entirety of the church out of proper authority—out of proper position beneath the feet of Jesus. We subconsciously get this concept because we talk about placing our sins and our problems in life "at the foot of the cross."

There is an Old Testament foreshadowing of this entire concept in the book of Ruth. Ruth was a Moabitess, the daughter-in-law of Naomi. Both were widows. Ruth gleaned in the field of Boaz, who turned out to be a relative of theirs. He was their kinsman redeemer. The kinsman redeemer was a male relative who had the privilege and responsibility to act on behalf of a needy member of his greater family. The eldest living male served as the kinsman redeemer when needed.

Naomi told Ruth to go lay at the feet of Boaz as he slept by his pile of grain on the threshing floor, and to do what he told her to do after that. Ruth 3:6–9 says,

> So she went down to the threshing floor
> and did according to all that her mother-in-law
> instructed her. And after Boaz had eaten and

drunk, and his heart was cheerful, he went to lie down at the end of the heap of grain; and she came softly, uncovered his feet, and lay down. Now it happened at midnight that the man was startled, and turned himself; and there, a woman was lying at his feet. And he said, "Who are you?" So she answered, "I am Ruth, your maidservant. Take your maidservant under your wing, for you are a close relative."

The men would use their prayer shawls as a covering over themselves, like a blanket. The two ends of the prayer shawl, which hung down over either arm when worn around the head/shoulders of a man, are called the wings. When a man spreads out his arms with a prayer shawl on, they look somewhat like the wings of a bird. It was Jewish practice for a groom to cover his bride with his prayer shawl during the wedding ceremony. He would hold it up and out over her head, as symbolic of his covering, his protection and shelter for his bride. Some translations say "skirt" instead of wing, but the Hebrew literal translation is wing. Ruth positioned herself at Boaz's feet. When Boaz noticed her, she asked him for his covering, his protection and shelter as his bride, asking Boaz to spread his wing over her. Ruth willingly placed herself, asking to be his bride, at his feet. She was putting him in a place of authority over her. Boaz did marry her, and she became the great-grandmother of King David, and is listed in the lineage of Y'shua in Matthew 1:5.

Jesus can be considered our kinsman redeemer since he came as a man and redeemed us because of our need that we could not solve on our own. Y'shua is our elder brother, as indicated in Hebrews 2:11: "For both He who sanctifies and those who are being sanctified are all of one, for which reason He is not ashamed to call them brethren." He redeems us by paying for our sins with His death. He takes us as His bride. He covers us with His blood, His protection, and calls us His family in Mark 3:33–35. This means that Jesus is over us in a position of authority, and we are at His feet.

When we do God's will from this position, we are victorious. Often, though, we get out of that proper position, and that gets us into trouble. I heard it described as having an umbrella over our head in the rain. Rebellion punches holes in that umbrella and lets the rain through. The umbrella does not protect us as much as it could if it did not have holes in it. Rebellion can also mean we step out from under that umbrella altogether, so we have no covering over our head in the rain, with the rain being the plans of the enemy to harm us. Sometimes, we don't realize we have gotten out of proper position, not meaning to do so.

For example, I had pernicious anemia. When I first developed it, I was so tired I literally had to hold my head up at the supper table. I was struggling to think and remember things. I couldn't spell "the" one day. I turned the wrong way on a divided highway one time while driving, which scared my son a lot. I went to the doctor and was diagnosed with pernicious anemia. For years, I had to give myself a monthly shot of vitamin B-12 in my muscles. I also had developed hypothyroidism years ago and had to take a pill every day. Years later, I finished reading Smith Wigglesworth's sermons on healing and finally understood that God really does heal people. I got it.

At that point, I was on a trip with my girlfriend and told her I was not going to take my monthly B-12 shot because I "got it" and understood that God healed me of pernicious anemia at the cross. She looked at me and advised me to not stop taking the thyroid medicine at the same time. Being the enthusiastic believer that I am, I ignored her warning. I did not tell my husband what I was doing because I didn't want to scare him. He worries about medical things. I planned to tell him a couple of months later that God had healed me when I could prove it to him. Before a couple of months went by, my body started to melt down. Literally. Half my face fell. I gained weight uncontrollably. My hair and skin became very dull. In short, I didn't like the way I looked in a mirror at all. I talked with another friend about this and told her that I had stopped taking both my B-12 shots and my thyroid medicine. She pointed out to me that I was out of proper position regarding authority since I did not tell my husband what I was doing. I went home and told him, and he made me go to the doctor. God did, indeed, heal me of pernicious anemia, and I have not taken another B-12 shot since. However, God did not heal my underactive thyroid, and I was dangerously low.

I had ignored God's warning about my thyroid, and I stepped out from under my physical authority, my husband, when I didn't tell him. Even though I didn't intend to deceive him because I did not discuss it with him and get his permission to stop taking the medicine, I got in trouble.

Sometimes we get it in our head that what we are doing must be God's will since the desire is so strong in us. However, there are checks and balances that God puts in place to help us stay in proper position regarding authority. A person who ignores the authority over them and continues to do their own will is often referred to as a "loose cannonball." In wooden warships that used cannons, a loose cannonball rolling around on deck was dangerous to all the sailors. It was also dangerous to the ship since it had enough weight that it could punch a hole in the side of the ship if sent rolling across the deck from a high wave. A very common "loose cannon" within the community of believers is a person who disagrees with a superior's decision at some point in time and decides to go around that decision, thinking they know better than the superior. I've learned that sometimes the "no" we don't want to hear from our authority is just God's training of us for future use.

Staying in position under the authority over us gives us the protection we need to effectively fight the enemy. When we are in proper position, the enemy can only attack us by going through the authority over us—Jesus. This weapon closes a lot of strategies that the enemy might try to use against us. If we stay aware of the deceptive methods he might use to talk us out from under that authority, we can render his plans to wreck us useless.

First John 5:14–15 says, "Now this is the confidence that we have in Him, that if we ask anything according to His will, He hears us. And if we know that He hears us, whatever we ask, we know that we have the petitions that we have asked of Him." The key is "according to His will." Daniel 11:32b says, "But the people who know their God shall be strong, and carry out great exploits." We need to know

God and to know His will. When we are willingly subject to His authority, when He tells us how to fight, we will be strong and carry out great exploits.

The story of David and Goliath is a great example of how staying in proper position under authority will produce great exploits for God's glory. David was tending to the sheep, according to his father Jesse's instructions. Three of his older brothers were with Saul at the big battle with the Philistines, and Jesse wanted to know how his sons were doing. First Samuel 17:17–20 says,

> Then Jesse said to his son David, "Take now…an ephah of this dried grain and these ten loaves, and run to your brothers at the camp… and see how your brothers fare, and bring back news of them"… So David rose early in the morning, left the sheep with a keeper, and took the things and went as Jesse had commanded him.

David was at the battle site because his father sent him there. Eliab, his eldest brother, got mad at David. In his anger, he disparaged David's work ethic, intent, and his character. He even mocked the financial status of his father. "And Eliab's anger was aroused against David, and he said, 'Why did you come down here? And with whom have you left those few sheep in the wilderness? I know your pride and the insolence of your heart, for you have come down to see the battle'" (1 Sam. 17:28). David's response was "What have I done now?" and he turned away from his brother to talk to other soldiers.

When you are under proper authority, some will try to talk you out of it. They will usually accuse you of exactly the opposite of what you are doing. That's a key to tell the source of that voice because if you are out from under proper authority, some who love you may tell you that. With both the enemy and God's voice basically telling you the same thing regarding your position under authority, the key is in the words. Eliab's words were slanderous and a lie. Since the devil can only lie (he is the father of all lies according to John 8:44) when he lies to you, he is telling you the exact opposite of the truth.

Eliab may have been the eldest son, but he was not an authority over David. Not being an authority over you will make some people mad. Be careful whom you allow to be in that position. This is a critical weapon of warfare, and Satan uses serious craftiness to try and steal this one from you.

David volunteered to fight Goliath, and the soldiers took him to King Saul: "And Saul said to David, 'Go, and the LORD be with you!" (1 Sam. 17:37b). Saul tried to help the effort by offering David his armor but allowed David to reject it. David went into the battle by the authority over all the Israelites, the king. Saul blessed David with "The LORD be with you!" It is very important for pastors to bless those intercessors who pray for their church. With blessing from authority, people praying can do great exploits in the spiritual realm.

This is also why it is important for men to bless the efforts of their wives, and parents to bless the efforts of their children. Because David operated under proper authority, he was able to defeat a giant with only one stone. David continued to experience great exploits because he continued to honor Saul as the authority, even though Saul's treatment of David deteriorated rapidly. David refused to harm Saul. David refused to avenge himself because of Saul's position of authority as king. Even if we cannot honor a person in a position of authority over us because of serious character flaws like Saul, we can honor the position of that authority. Saul became abusive of David; he even tried to kill David numerous times. David removed himself from Saul's presence. He fled for his life, but he still continued to honor Saul as king the entire time Saul was pursuing him to kill him. David honored Saul even upon hearing of his death.

I think the best way to tell if we are staying in proper submission and position to the authority over us is to carefully and honestly analyze our attitude. In my health meltdown, my attitude was subtle arrogance. I thought I would protect my husband from his fears regarding health issues by telling him after the fact that I had stopped my medicines. In essence, I was acting like I was better because I wasn't afraid. If we think we know better than our authority, we're looking at getting out of position if we continue on that path. We may offer our opinion and wisdom to the authority over us, if they ask for it, but then we leave the ultimate decision to them.

If they are wrong, then the issue is between them and God, and you are not in that issue because you were obedient to the authority God placed over you. First Timothy 4:7b–8 says, "And exercise yourself toward godliness…godliness is profitable for all things, having promise of the life that now is and of that which is to come." Godliness can also be translated reverence. I decided for myself what my husband's reaction would be, decided it didn't match what I wanted to do, and therefore discarded his authority by not even having the conversation with him. I did not honor him by giving him the opportunity to tell me himself what his opinion was.

Paul's prayer for believers in Ephesians 3:14–20 starts with position: "For this reason I bow my knees to the Father." He willingly subjected himself to God our Father by kneeling in prayer. Paul continued this prayer: "For this reason I bow my knees to the Father of our Lord Jesus Christ, from whom the whole family in heaven and earth is named." Paul is appealing to God the Father on behalf of every reader of his letter to Ephesus. Why is Paul praying this way?

> That He would grant you, according to the riches of His glory, to be strengthened with might through His Spirit in the inner man, that Christ may dwell in your hearts through faith; that you, being rooted and grounded in love, may be able to comprehend with all the saints what is the width and length and depth and height—to know the love of Christ which passes knowledge; that you may be filled with all the fullness of God. Now to Him who is able to do exceedingly abundantly above all that we ask or think, according to the power that works in us, to Him be glory in the church by Christ Jesus to all generations forever and ever. Amen. (Eph. 3:14–21)

Paul is praying from this position of subjection to proper authority so that we, as believers, would realize and utilize (seize) all the riches available to us, through God's immeasurable love for us, to accomplish all the great exploits He had planned before creation for us to accomplish.

Knowing God's love for us and the power He has made available to us to accomplish His will on Earth is a source of great peace, faith, hope, and joy for every believer. Being in proper position under authority is a very powerful weapon in our belt of truth.

8

Sixth Weapon: Attitude

In a televised golf tournament, teams were made up of an amateur player with a professional player. On one particular team, the amateur's dad, to honor his son's success in golf, was walking through the crowd along each hole as his son was playing the course. The amateur hit an incredible drive on a par 5. The professional playing with him turned to him and said something to the effect of "Wow! With a drive like that, you have to go for the green on your second shot!" That's really strong praise and encouragement from someone who is a professional. The amateur pulled out a long club to go for the green and happened to look over toward his father in the crowd. He saw his dad shaking his head no. The amateur hit the shot, and it went into the water in front of the green.

As I discussed in the last chapter, it is important to know who is your authority. In this case, the professional teammate (and team leader) was the authority over the amateur golfer for the time they were playing together on the course. While the amateur player obviously loves and honors his father, the father wasn't invited into the strategy session between team members on the fairway, yet he rendered an opinion anyway. His negative opinion planted doubts into the player's mind, which deflated the enthusiastic "You can do it!" from the team leader. That, in my opinion, deflated his swing just enough to miss the mark. The amateur player had conflicting attitudes vying for his mind. One was positive, and one was negative.

Guarding our attitude is just as important as knowing who is our authority and staying in proper position to that authority. All athletes will tell you a lot of the game is played in the mind. Our mindset, our attitude, is critical to being a successful soldier in God's army.

Look at David's attitude before his fight with Goliath: "For who is this uncircumcised Philistine, that he should defy the armies of the living God?" (1 Sam. 17:26). David's confidence is seen again in verse 32: "Then David said to Saul, 'Let no man's heart fail because of him; your servant will go and fight with this Philistine.'" David is offended on God's account that Goliath is taunting God's army and profaning God's Name. He is confident he can defeat this giant based on what he's already accomplished:

> When a lion or a bear came and took a lamb out the flock, I went out after it and struck it, and delivered the lamb from its mouth; and when it arose against me, I caught it by its beard, and struck and killed it. Your servant has killed both lion and bear; and this uncircumcised Philistine will be like one of them, seeing he has defied the armies of the living God.

Moreover David said, "The LORD, who delivered me from the paw of the lion and from the paw of the bear, He will deliver me from the hand of this Philistine" (1 Sam. 17:34–37).

Notice that David was close enough to the lion and the bear that they rose against David. He was close enough to grab them by their beards, which means their teeth were very close to David's face and body. If David was close enough to grab them below their mouth, he also was well within range of their paws and claws. A bear or lion close enough to be grabbed in this way would have probably taken David up in the air as they raised on their hind legs, assuming David had the strength to hang on. That would be a pretty intense battle and qualifies in the life-and-death category. Based on his past experiences, battling a giant was no scarier than what he had already been through. David was confident of his abilities. David was also confident of his God, the LORD.

David did not allow the negative talk from his eldest brother to disturb his confidence. First Samuel 17:45–47 says,

> Then David said to the Philistine, "You come to me with a sword, with a spear, and with a javelin. But I come to you in the name of the LORD of hosts, the God of the armies of Israel, whom you have defied. This day the LORD will deliver you into my hand, and I will strike you and take your head from you. And this day I will give the carcasses of the camp of the Philistines to the birds of the air and the wild beasts of the earth, that all the earth may know that there is a God in Israel. Then all this assembly shall know that the LORD does not save with sword and spear; for the battle is the LORD's, and He will give you into our hands."

David had confidence in himself and the LORD and was willing to say so out loud.

In Zechariah 4:6–7, Zechariah heard the Word of God saying to him: "This is the word of the LORD to Zerubbabel: 'Not by might, nor by power, but by My Spirit, says the LORD of hosts. Who are you, O great mountain? Before Zerubbabel you shall become a plain!'" LORD of hosts is God's title as leader of His army. Y'shua taught His disciples about moving a mountain too. Mark 11:22–25 says,

> So Jesus answered and said to them, "Have faith in God. For assuredly, I say to you, whoever says to this mountain, 'Be removed and be cast into the sea,' and does not doubt in his heart, but believes that those things he says will be done, he will have whatever he says. Therefore I say to you, whatever things you ask when you pray,

believe that you receive them, and you will have
them. And whenever you stand praying, if you
have anything against anyone, forgive him, that
your Father in heaven may also forgive you your
trespasses."

God tells us we can make mountains into plains (solve huge
problems or messes in our lives or the lives of others) not in our own
strength, but by the power of His Spirit. Jesus taught that our attitude about the process will determine our victory. He also warned
that attitudes about others will also impact our success. If we have
unforgiveness in our hearts toward anyone, our prayers will be hin-
dered. David had a history of verbal attacks from his eldest brother,
if not all his brothers. His father overlooked him while he was tending sheep to parade all his other sons before Samuel. Samuel sanctified Jesse and his sons and invited them to the sacrifice. Apparently,
David was not involved in that. It seemed that Jesse only remembered his youngest son when Samuel asked him if all his sons were
there. When Eliab attacked David at the army camp against Goliath,
David's reaction was "What have I done now?" This indicates that he
had been attacked many times in the past by his brother. David could
have had unforgiveness, resentment, or hardness of heart toward this
angry older brother and maybe toward his whole family, but he chose
to just ignore his brother instead. He did not let his experiences with
his family influence how he thought in this instance.

Sometimes it is hard to know if you have a hard heart toward
another person. In a very lengthy and unfriendly business transac-
tion, my husband was placed under extreme stress. The opposing
side had decided to put pressure on us via public press. I had to guard
my heart against taking up offense on behalf of my husband. I prayed
and forgave the ones publicly saying all the untrue and negative
things about my husband. After my morning prayer time, I would
pick up the newspaper and read another story of untruth against my
husband. I would be right back where I was before prayers. My pastor's wife suggested I stop reading the paper, which I promptly did. It
was hard to work through the offense and hardening of heart against

the people coming against my husband. I learned a trick to show me where my heart was, and here it is:

If God is bringing someone to your mind while reading this, stop right now and immediately pray for that person. Pray right now that God blesses that person in specific ways, and pray blessings on them. Is it difficult for you to find words to pray? Is it hard to think of specific blessings you are asking God to place on them? If it is, you probably have a hard heart against that person and need to deal with God about it. Remember that forgiving a person for the harm they did to you is not agreeing that they had the right to harm you. It is not equal to saying that what they did to you was okay, or right, or even permissible. However, holding onto that grudge, hardness, resentment, or offense is equal to telling God that you know justice better than He does. It is also putting you in a place of arrogance in that you are, in essence, saying that your hurt is greater than any others and needs to be held onto longer. To get to a place where you can truly and genuinely pray for blessings on that other person, list each specific offense, hurt, betrayal, etc. to God. Specifically say you forgive them for that. Then release that person to God's care. Only God will know whether ultimate repentance from that person is possible. He may choose mercy if repentance is coming, or He may choose justice. There are always consequences to sinful behavior, even if God forgives us as we repent.

If you are seeking to sincerely get rid of all hardness of heart against someone, God will help you. My husband was involved in another business. This business partner demanded to buy the entire business for only what he could afford to pay. This was significantly less than what we had invested in it and what it was worth. After much prayer and negotiation, the partner did buy our portion of the business. I had hurt and resentment in my heart since I felt like we were robbed of a significant amount of money. I kept bringing the issue to God in prayer, often with tears because I know it is not God's will to carry hurt and resentment in our hearts. I thought I had conquered the problem until I was talking with someone about that situation. As we talked, I realized I still had shades of resentment left.

I asked them to pray for me. I also asked God to help me get rid of all hurt and resentment.

A few days later, I was listening to a prayer conference call. One caller asked for help since he was struggling with his attitude. He also owned a business, and people were stealing from him regularly. He didn't know what to do. One of the leaders on the conference call told him the victory was in his attitude. If he changed his attitude, he could change his heart. Instead of looking at the problem as someone stealing, he said to consider the loss as a gift from the owner to the thief. In doing that, he reminded the owner he would then be sowing and could then spiritually place a demand based on the principle of sowing and reaping. He could expect a spiritual return of some sort from God as he reaped from what he had decided to sow. I knew that was my answer! I immediately prayed to God, giving to the previous business owner what I had up to that moment considered my loss. It was now a gift. I asked God to consider that gift as my sowing into the kingdom and asked for a harvest I could reap from it. I left all the details up to God. I had perfect peace as a result of that prayer. I felt such a release and knew all hurt and the last bits of resentment were truly gone from my heart.

This was important to me because we were en route to an overseas ministry trip. I wanted a clean heart before arriving. God gave it to me. While on the trip, that business owner's wife emailed me, and we arranged to meet. I had not talked with her in several years. We had a long talk, and I was actually able to minister to her in a different area of her life. We now have a precious friendship reestablished. The harvest I realized from this act of changing my attitude is very precious to me and worth way more than the financial amount I had considered lost and decided to give away. Forgiveness is crucial in the kingdom of God. Jesus tells us in Matthew 6:14–15 that our forgiveness by our Father God is dependent upon our forgiveness of others. It is that important in the kingdom. It is not optional; it is mandatory.

Sometimes, I realize that it takes time to work through the hurt, anger, resentment, bitterness, and forgiveness. Here is another tactic I have successfully used. God says in Ezekiel 11:19 that He will take our stony heart out of us and give us a new heart of flesh. A stony heart is a hard heart. Anger, bitterness, resentment, etc. are all emotions that make our hearts hard. I have at times had to grit my teeth and confess with my mouth what I knew was God's will—to forgive, to praise instead of complain, or whatever the situation warranted. I knew God's desire for my attitude and my behavior. So I would confess that with my mouth. I then freely admitted to God that He and I both knew my heart was not in alignment with the words I obediently proclaimed with my mouth. However, I gave Him my heart and gave Him permission to change it. That is His business, not mine. He is in the business of changing hearts. That is what He wrote in His Scriptures. I then continued to praise and pray in tongues until I felt the change happen. I felt the change from obedient praise to genuine praise, for example. In other cases, I felt the anger leave and forgiveness and love flood in.

David had a positive attitude and did not allow his brother's words to affect him. Let's look at another example of a positive attitude in the book of Joshua. Rahab lived in Jericho and hid the Israelite spies on her roof among stalks of flax. The king of Jericho heard that spies came into her house and ordered her to bring forth the men. To protect the Israelites, she denied that they were in her house. She then told the two spies,

> I know that the LORD has given you the land, that the terror of you has fallen on us, and that all the inhabitants of the land are faint-hearted because of you...our hearts melted; neither did there remain any more courage in anyone because of you, for the LORD your God, He is God in heaven above and on earth beneath. Now therefore, I beg you, swear to me by the LORD, since I have shown you kindness, that you also will show kindness to my father's house, and give me a true token, and spare...and deliver our lives from death. (Josh. 2:9–13)

The spies agreed to save her and everyone under her roof, if she hung a scarlet cord from her window when the Israelites returned to conquer the city. "Then she let them down by a rope through the window, for her house was on the city wall; she dwelt on the wall... And she sent them away and they departed. And she bound the scarlet cord in the window" (Josh. 2:15 and 21b).

Rahab had an interesting attitude. She could have given in to fear since all the people of the land were in great fear of the Israelites. She also could have potentially gained some status with the king of Jericho by turning the spies over to the king. Instead, she acknowledged that the God of Israel was the one true God. The Hebrew word translated "rope" that Rahab used to let the spies down the wall to escape from Jericho actually means a twisted rope, especially a measuring line: by implication, a measured inheritance, according to *Strong's Concordance*. She was asking for the lives of her entire family. She was asking for a measure of inheritance with the Israelites. She was asking for salvation for her and her entire family.

After Rahab let the two men down the wall outside the city, she bound the scarlet cord in the window. She did not wait until she thought they would be back. In fact, she knew at that time she had at least three days wait since she advised them to head to the mountains and hide themselves for three days there before going their way. Imagine the situation: the king already knew the men went into her house. He sent men out to pursue after them while immediately shutting the gate behind them so the two spies would be trapped inside the city if they had not left. His men came back empty handed. The king of Jericho had to have been suspicious and probably was watching Rahab's house, just in case. Now, suddenly the same night they were looking for spies, she hung a scarlet line out the window of her house. This line would have had to be significant in size. The Israelite troops would have to be able to see it so as not to slay those inside that particular house. This line was much larger than just a scarlet thread or string. If it was going to be big enough to be visible in the midst of battle, it was certainly large enough for the people of Jericho to also see it. It was hanging out the window and down the outside portion of the walls of Jericho. The king's men certainly would have seen it. If they did not interrogate her about it, they certainly would have been watching her quite closely.

Yet Rahab kept her mind set on seeking for salvation. She did not waver. She did not allow fear, pressure, and intense scrutiny to change her attitude. The word in Hebrew used for the scarlet "cord" that she hung from her window figuratively means "expectancy—expectation, hope, live, thing that I long for," according to *Strong's*. The root of that word means "to bind together by twisting...gather together...patiently tarry, wait (for, on upon)." When Rahab hung that scarlet cord out the window and down the wall, she was patiently, expectantly waiting to be taken into the nation of Israel. She was waiting for her entire family's lives to be spared.

In looking at Scripture, Rahab had at least three weeks of waiting, and maybe more. The spies went to the mountain, hid for three days, then came down the mountain and went to their camp. They then camped just across the Jordan for three days, not counting the number of days it took them to move camp. The entire nation of Israel all crossed the Jordan, and then all the males were circumcised and rested in camp until they were healed. This healing period could take anywhere for seven to ten days up to six to eight weeks for adult men. They also celebrated Passover and marched silently around Jericho for six days before the final battle day. Rahab kept that scarlet cord hanging out her window and down the wall the entire time.

It is also important to note that the walls of Jericho fell, but Joshua told the two men to go into Rehab's house and from there bring out Rahab and all her family members that were with her, as they had promised her. "And the young men who had been spies went in and brought out Rahab, her father, her mother, her brothers, and all that she had" (Josh. 6:23). Apparently, Rahab's house on the wall did not collapse with the rest of the wall. Rahab and her family were safe inside her house, and the two men were able to go into the house and lead them all out safely. Because she was trusting in the God of Israel, even if she did not know Him very well, Rahab and her family survived in her house which still stood on the wall. Her portion of the walls of Jericho may have been the only one to survive. An entire city was trashed and flattened, but Rahab's house survived.

In my imagination, I can see her house standing on a section of wall that survived intact. It may have looked like a tower with the rest of the wall toppled down.

"He is the tower of salvation to His king, and shows mercy to His anointed, to David and his descendants forevermore" (2 Sam. 22:51).

"The LORD is my rock and my fortress and my deliverer; my God, my strength, in whom I will trust; my shield and the horn of my salvation, my stronghold" (Ps. 18:2). A stronghold is also a tower.

"The name of the LORD is a strong tower; The righteous run into it and are safe" (Prov. 18:10).

Rahab's positive attitude, patience, and determination saved her family. Was her positive attitude important to God? Her name is listed in the genealogy of Y'shua in Matthew 1:5–6: "Salmon begot Boaz by Rahab, Boaz begot Obed by Ruth, Obed begot Jesse, and Jesse begot David the king." Rahab was the mother of Boaz, who married Ruth. She was the great, great grandmother of King David. David wrote the first two verses quoted above, and David's son Solomon wrote the verse from Proverbs. I can image that the story of Rahab's rescue was told and retold at family gatherings so that David, as a child, also heard the history of his ancestor's rescue by the scarlet cord hanging out the window, leading to a love story of marriage.

For us today as believers, it really is all about our attitude. We can look at things and see a glass half empty or half full: same glass, same amount of liquid in the glass in both cases. The only difference is perspective, or attitude. A half empty glass perspective looks at all the things going wrong in our lives, or in our country, or in our world. We can focus on how horrible things are. For a "glass half full" perspective, God wants us to see things His way. God is still in charge. He wants us to pray, praise, and preserve others. God wants us to be the testimony of Jesus to the lost world with the light He has put inside each one of us. Our joy, our love for others, our care and compassion for the lost and their sorrows bring Jesus into every situation. We can love, have joy, praise and have hope because God has it all in control! It is not just salvation for others; it is living supernaturally.

The equal amount of liquid in the glass in either case can be considered the power of God available for us to utilize. Some bemoan the fact that the liquid (God's power) used already wasn't enough to solve all the problems and ignore the liquid still available to be used. God wants us to see the power of God as unlimited, available, and expected for us to use.

God did something awesome to illustrate this concept for me in my prayer time on my porch. The sky was totally clouded over. No blue sky was apparent anywhere—just piles of clouds on top of each other and seemingly piled in layers all the way to the horizon. As I was looking at all the clouds, suddenly the sun was shining! There was a bright area in the clouds and sunlight was streaming onto our porch. However, I could not see the sun, nor could I even see a beam of light. The one section of clouds was bright, but no sun was visible. Yet sunlight was clearly hitting me where I sat. It seemed impossible to be sitting in a stream of sunlight with a completely clouded over sky. His point: Only God can do the seemingly impossible.

We can control our attitude. We need to remember that there is always blue sky behind or above the clouds. Back to the amateur golfer I talked about at the beginning of this chapter, he had a choice to make in his thought process at that point. One choice was to be cautious, carefully considering risk management and course strategy. This is a negative mindset. The other choice was just to go for the green. To win big, you have to be willing to risk big too. David could have considered that he might lose against Goliath, but he was not counting only on his strength. He relied on the LORD, knowing that the LORD had helped him win battles against the bear and the lion. Rahab could have waited to hang the scarlet cord out her window, living cautiously so she did not bring the notice of the king of Jericho further on her household. However, she would have risked not getting the cord out the window in time since she did not know exactly when they would come back. The longer she waited, the more she could have allowed negative thoughts in: fear, hesitation, questioning the word of the men or even if they intended to come back at all. She could have given in to those negative thoughts and pulled the cord back in. She did not alter her attitude: she kept the cord out the window and trusted the God of Israel for her life.

If you find yourself with a negative attitude, here are some tools to help you change it:

1. Spend some time in prayer listing out loud (or on a sheet of paper so it is visible to you) all the things for which you are grateful to God. Be very specific, like "I am grateful for sunshine"; "I thank you, God, for my bed"; "I am grateful to you, God, for my clothes"; "I thank you, God, for blue skies"; etc.

2. If your attitude is against someone you are supposed to love, like a spouse or relative, spend time in prayer listing to God every good thing they have done for you, their good attributes, etc.

3. Do the same thing for anyone else about whom you have a bad attitude. Ask God to give you His perspective on that person. Ask to see that person the way God sees them. Visualize them and say, "You are so precious to our Father! He loves you so much!"

4. Develop a list of prayer requests that God has already answered. It is good to keep a book, with requests listed on one side of the page, and the answers on the other. I was feeling defeated one day—like God did not hear my prayers at all. I happened to find an old book of prayer requests from several years before. One request was for a woman who came to prayer meeting with ovarian cancer. On the other side of the page, I had written "answered" but did not write down details. The day after finding that old prayer journal I again saw that very same woman, who was visiting our church. I had not seen her in several years. I asked her how God had answered our prayers. She said, "Don't you remember? God totally healed me!" That really turned my mumbly-grump attitude back into a joyous one and boosted my attitude about prayer too.

5. Begin praising God. Sing praise songs or choruses or make your own up.

6. Pray in tongues. I lived in a house where the kitchen was very difficult to work in. It was large, but the original owners who built the house redesigned the kitchen, and I would guess without the help of an architect. Cabinets were three feet long, with a six-inch door only at the corner of the space, which made it very difficult to find anything in the cabinets. The floor was so old the top layer of the vinyl flooring was completely gone. My feet stuck to it when I walked because I was walking on the inner layer. The kitchen sink and garbage disposal backed up on a regular basis because there were improper angles to the drain under the sink. One night I was home alone, and the garbage disposal backed up at the same time the dishwasher started to drain. The trap under the sink fell down from the pressure of the water. Within a minute or so, I was ankle-deep in icky water flooding the kitchen floor. The water was also dripping through the kitchen floor down onto the carpet in the room below the kitchen. I had to clean up the mess myself. I got a mop and bucket, and while I was mopping and throwing water down a different drain, I prayed. "Father, Your Word says to praise in all situations, so I am going to praise out of obedience. I am going to pray and sing to you, because Your Word says to do that in all situations. You and I both know my heart is not into this, but You also promise in Jeremiah and Ezekiel to give me a new heart. So as I obey with my mouth, I am trusting You to change my heart and get my heart to line up with my words." I started out gritting my teeth while praising and praying in tongues, singing new songs to Him. By the time I was done mopping and washing the floor and taking care of the carpet downstairs, I really was singing out of a worshipping heart full of joy. God had changed my heart and aligned it with my words.

I had a choice in regard to my attitude. I chose obedience to the Word, and God changed my attitude. The cleanup may have actually taken over an hour, but it did not feel like that to me. I was caught up in worshipping God and didn't mind the time doing something that was not on my original to-do list for the evening.

Ephesians 1:3 says, "Blessed be the God and Father of our Lord Jesus Christ, who has blessed us with every spiritual blessing in the heavenly places in Christ." The word *spiritual* means supernatural. God, Father of our Lord Jesus Christ, has blessed (He has already done it!) us with every supernatural blessing in Christ. According to John 17:21 and 23, Jesus is in the Father, the Father is in Jesus, Jesus is in us, and we are in Jesus and the Father. That's quite a mouthful, but just as God the Father, God the Son, and God the Holy Spirit is a triune God—like a triangle: One God, but three distinct points or aspects revealed to us—Jesus is describing here another triangle composed of Father, Son, and believers. Since we are in Christ, where is Christ? He is seated at the right hand of the Father. That means we are also seated at the right hand of the Father. By the mystery of God, we are both places—heaven and Earth—at the same time. We just are not as aware of heaven. The blessings are heavenly blessings, but that doesn't mean they are for us once we get up to heaven. Why would we need God's power and blessings there? Heaven is perfection. We need those things down here. The Lord's prayer, speaking of the Father's will, says, "Your will be done on earth as it is in heaven." Let it be on Earth as it already is in heaven.

Since we are in Christ, John 14:30 records Jesus saying, "The ruler of this world...has nothing in me." There was no sin in Jesus, so Satan had no place to hook his claws into Him. Satan had no entry to attack Jesus. He tried to tempt Him. It was God's plan for Jesus to be tortured and crucified. Where are we? We are in Christ. What was Christ's attitude like? Love, patience, kindness, gentleness, obedience to the Father, joy, peace, zeal for His Father's House. Jesus had a positive attitude at all times. He did not walk in fear, worry, or negative thoughts. We can do the same with God's help.

SIXTH WEAPON: ATTITUDE

A positive, steadfast, grateful attitude because of God in your life makes it possible to achieve great exploits for God's glory. Some battles may be prolonged, some may be long, but many will be as easy as fishing in a bucket of fish. Guard your attitude. Keep it positive, and be full of faith, hope, and joy because we serve a mighty God who has given us this weapon hanging on our belt of truth.

9

SEVENTH WEAPON: PATIENCE

"Patience is a virtue" is a proverbial statement that I grew up hearing. It actually has been traced to a poem written by William Langland in 1377. It can be traced further back to an epic poem written in the early fifth century.

"Have patience, have patience, don't be in such a hurry," sang Psalty the Singing Psalm Book to children. Our children did not appreciate it when my husband or I started singing that same phrase to them when they were not exhibiting patience. It usually elicited a groan from them, although they loved the Psalty videos and cassette tapes.

"Don't pray for patience!" everyone told me as a new Christian. They chuckled and implied God would give me many trials and situations where I could choose frustration or patience. However, I wanted and needed patience. I was like a racehorse when it came to God's timing. Sometimes, I would hear Him give me some instruction, and off to the races I went. I didn't wait for the gate to open and the race to officially begin. I bolted out of the gate and was ahead of God's timing. It messed things up when I did that. I had to learn patience and wait for God's timing before I acted upon what He told me.

In our harried, stressed, ultra-busy world of today, we want to check things off our list, get this project done, complete that task and get on to the next one. We've become shortsighted and task focused rather than goal-at-the-end-of-the-race focused.

What does patience mean? According to *Strong's Concordance*, *patience* means "cheerful endurance, constancy, patient continuance (waiting)." It is from a root word that means "stay under (behind), remain, to undergo or bear trials, have fortitude." So when we cheerfully endure or walk in constancy in our walk with God, we are exhibiting patience. If you take the root word from which patience comes, it means if we stay under Jesus, behind Him, and bear our trials, having fortitude, we are exhibiting patience.

It is a powerful weapon of warfare against the enemy's tactics. There are several examples of patience in the Bible. These examples kept the long-term focus of what they were to do for God and did not waver from that despite feelings of frustration every once in a while.

Moses is one example of patience. We often think that Moses went up Mount Sinai, received the Ten Commandments, and life went on. Let's look at the details of exactly what Moses was required to do. Exodus 19:3 records, "Then Moses went up to God." Once up the mountain, God gave Moses a promise for the people: "Now... if you will indeed obey My voice and keep My covenant, then you shall be a special treasure to Me above all people; for all the earth is Mine. And you shall be to Me a kingdom of priests and a holy nation" (verses 5–6). So Moses went down to the people in verse 7 and told them what God said. "So Moses came and called for the elders of the people, and laid before them all these words which the Lord commanded him."

At this point, Moses had hiked up and down Mount Sinai. He is eighty-plus years old. Mount Sinai is 7,497 feet tall, or 2,285 meters. Today, there are two paths to hike up the mountain. The longer but shallower path takes two and a half hours with coffee houses along the way. The steeper path is harder. Exodus 19:8 says, "So Moses brought back the words of the people to the Lord." To receive the Word of the Lord for the people he is leading, to give it to them, and to take their answer back to God required Moses to be hiking for seven and a half hours up, down, and up the mountain.

His job didn't end there, though. In Exodus 19:10–14, Moses goes down to the people again: "Then the LORD said to Moses, 'Go to the people and consecrate them…' So Moses went down from the mountain to the people, and sanctified the people." This meant another two-and-a-half-hour trip down the mountain to do so (this is assuming an eighty-plus-year-old man was walking at the average pace of today's climbers via today's pathways).

It continues: "Then it came to pass on the third day, in the morning…the LORD called Moses to the top of the mountain, and Moses went up" (verses 16 and 20). As soon as Moses got to the top of the mountain (two and a half hours later, again assuming he could trek at modern pace), "And the LORD said to Moses, 'Go down and warn the people.'" Moses exhibited a bit of resistance to this command and said the people wouldn't come up Mount Sinai because the Lord had already warned them. But the LORD replied and told him again to go down: "So Moses went down to the people and spoke to them" (verse 25).

Are you getting tired just reading about all the hiking Moses did? It is implied that Moses went back up between Exodus 19:25 and Exodus 20:1 where he begins to receive the Ten Commandments. To recap, Moses went up to God, Moses came down to the people, Moses went up to God, Moses went down to the people, Moses went up to God, Moses went down to the people, and Moses went up to God, then of course came down with the tablets of the Ten Commandments.

In chapter 24, Moses was told to come up to the Lord in verse 1. In verse 3, Moses told the people all the LORD's words and laws. In Exodus 24:9, Moses went up with 70 elders, Aaron, Nadab and Abihu. They saw the God of Israel: "They saw God, and they ate and drank" (verse 11). Moses went higher on the mountain and had to wait a week for God.

> Then Moses went up into the mountain,
> and a cloud covered the mountain. Now the
> glory of the LORD rested on Mount Sinai, and
> the cloud covered it six days. And on the seventh

day He called to Moses out of the midst of the
cloud... And Moses was on the mountain forty
days and forty nights. (Verses 15–18)

This is a great example of patience. Moses kept ascending and
descending the mountain, at great physical effort and time, with the
long-term sight of leading the people according to God's direction.
He exhibited constancy, fortitude, and patient continuance.

What happens when we don't have patience? What happened to
the people? A golden calf! They were afraid, having seen the smoke
and lightning and having heard the voice of God thunder. They told
Moses to go, being so afraid they thought they would die: "Now
all the people witnessed the thunderings, the lightning flashes, the
sound of the trumpet, and the mountain smoking; and when the
people saw it, they trembled and stood afar off. Then they said to
Moses, 'You speak with us, and we will hear; but let not God speak
with us, lest we die'" (Exod. 20:18–19). God displayed some of His
power to put the fear of God in them and keep them from sinning,
according to the next verse.

However, the people did not have patience to wait for Moses
to come down from the mountain: "Now when the people saw that
Moses delayed coming down from the mountain, the people gath-
ered together to Aaron, and said to him, 'Come, make us gods that
shall go before us; for as for this Moses, the man who brought us up
out of the land of Egypt, we do not know what has become of him'"
(Exod. 32:1). They had witnessed God's power on their behalf at the
Red Sea. They had just proclaimed they would listen to and obey
Moses because God was so awesome they were afraid they would die.
Yet they immediately turned their back to God and rejected Him.
They ordered their priest to create gods for them to follow. They
didn't even have the patience to wait forty days and forty nights.

If God has given you a word, a promise, a vision for the future,
or a dream, don't let go of it! Hang on, remind yourself of that word,
or promise, or vision, or dream. It will come to pass if we persevere
and have patience. If we give up before it is fulfilled, Satan has won.
He knows that, so he sends discouragement, hopelessness, despair,

oppression, aggravation, irritation, or whatever else he thinks will cause us to give up before God's perfect time of fulfillment of His plan in our life. Don't be hasty to create a golden calf to solve your problem. It won't help. If you have to carve your god yourself, it won't help you at all. It can't.

Leading people can be very frustrating. Raising a family can be very frustrating. Whether it is one child, twelve children, or a couple million people, leaders of people need patience. We all need patience when dealing with others. Without patience, we cannot honor others or respect them. Both of those are things God wants us to do because honor and respect are part of love. God wants us to love others. Love requires patience. Moses and God both had their moments of frustration. When Aaron made the golden calf, the Lord told Moses, to paraphrase, "*Your* children, whom *you* brought out of Egypt, have sinned." Moses responded, "Oh, no, they're *your* children! *You* brought them up out of Egypt." Like a hot potato, the Lord and Moses were tossing ownership of leadership back and forth. This is an indication of how hard leadership is.

In Numbers 11, the people were wailing because they missed meat. They were tired of eating manna every day and longed for the foods available in Egypt. Gluttony was winning the battle for their minds and their souls. Moses heard all the wailing, and went to the Lord in prayer:

> Why have You afflicted Your servant? And why have I not found favor in Your sight, that You have laid the burden of all these people on me?... I am not able to bear all these people alone... If You treat me like this, please kill me here and now—if I have found favor in Your sight—and do not let me see my wretchedness! (Num. 11:11–15)

Yet even in frustration, he still interceded for the people's lives when God wanted to destroy them for their sinful behavior and attitudes. Moses kept his eyes on the long-term promises of God and, in patience, led the people toward that promise.

Jeremiah is another example of patience. He was called as a young man to prophesy to his people for forty years. Their hard hearts and sinful behavior caused their situation to deteriorate over all that time. Yet Jeremiah kept on delivering the messages of the Lord to the people with patience. Heartbroken over what he saw and heard, he continued to hold out God's loving calls of repentance and promise to the people who had turned their backs to God.

Jeremiah delivered the messages, and by chapter 11, the men of Anathoth decided to kill him. That is a hostile audience. Even then, Jeremiah took his problem to the Lord rather than confront the men who desired to kill him:

> Now the LORD gave me knowledge of it, and I know it; for You showed me their doings. But I was like a docile lamb brought to the slaughter; and I did not know that they had devised schemes against me, saying, "Let us destroy the tree with its fruit, and let us cut him off from the land of the living, that his name may be remembered no more..." Therefore thus says the LORD concerning the men of Anathoth who seek your life. (Jer. 11:18–23)

The amazing part of this situation was that Jeremiah was from the group of priests who were in Anathoth (Jer. 1:1). These were people who lived in the town he lived in and may have been priests from the school that Jeremiah had come from. Sometimes the greatest patience is required for those who are closest to you.

In chapter 13, God told Jeremiah to hide a sash by the Euphrates River. That does not seem like such a hard thing to do until you realize how far it was to the Euphrates River. God asked Jeremiah to do a prophetic act to create a "picture" of what the Lord wanted His people to know. Jeremiah had been prophesying in and around Jerusalem and Judah. The Euphrates River is 722 miles, or 1,162 kilometers, from Jerusalem. It is not recorded how Jeremiah got to the river. Assuming he walked (which was the common method of transportation, especially for the poor) a fast pace of walking is four miles per hour. If he could walk twelve hours a day, he would have walked forty-eight miles each day. At that pace, it would have taken fifteen days to get to the Euphrates River from Jerusalem. Then, it would have taken him fifteen days to return. At the more normal pace of three miles per hour, this trip would have been twenty days one way. That is assuming he could walk for twelve hours a day.

"And the word of the Lord came to me the second time, saying, 'Take the sash that you acquired, which is around your waist, and arise, go to the Euphrates, and hide it there in a hole in the rock.' So I went and hid it by the Euphrates, as the Lord commanded me" (Jer. 13:3–5). The next verses say that God called him to return to the Euphrates to retrieve the sash: "Now it came to pass after many days that the Lord said to me, 'Arise, go to the Euphrates, and take from there the sash which I commanded you to hide there.' Then I went to the Euphrates and dug, and I took the sash from the place where I had hidden it; and there was the sash, ruined. It was profitable for nothing." That was another month or month and a half of walking to complete this task—all for a "picture" to accompany the word that God gave Jeremiah to speak to the people, including the king and the queen mother.

Jeremiah next encountered false prophets who spoke the opposite of Jeremiah's prophesies to the people, and to Jeremiah. He took his concerns to the Lord in Jeremiah 14:13–14:

> Then I said, "Ah, Lord God! Behold, the prophets say to them, 'You shall not see the sword, nor shall you have famine, but I will give you assured peace in this place.' And the Lord said to me, 'The prophets prophesy lies in My name. I have not sent them, commanded them, nor spoken to them; they prophesy to you a false vision, divination, a worthless thing, and the deceit of their heart.'"

Jeremiah had a tough job. God knew it and told Jeremiah in 15:20, "'And I will make you to this people a fortified bronze wall; and they will fight against you, but they shall not prevail against you; for I am with you to save you and deliver you,' says the LORD." God equipped Jeremiah for the persecution, rejection, and hatred that were coming against him because of God's words coming out of his mouth. God gave Jeremiah the fortitude (patience) to continue his work on behalf of God and the people.

In Jeremiah 18:18, men devised a plot to slander Jeremiah. By chapter 20, verses 1–2, Jeremiah was physically hit and put in stocks for doing what God told him to do: "Now Pashhur the son of Immer, the priest who was also chief governor in the house of the LORD, heard that Jeremiah prophesied these things. Then Pashhur struck Jeremiah the prophet, and put him in the stocks that were in the high gate of Benjamin, which was by the house of the LORD." Jeremiah was in stocks for twenty-four hours. Yet Jeremiah continued to endure and obeyed God with constancy, never wavering in his obedience.

Not all the people were too sinful to repent. When we operate in faithful patience, lives are saved:

> Thus says the LORD, the God of Israel: "Like these good figs, so will I acknowledge those who are carried away captive from Judah, whom I have sent out of this place for their own good, into the land of the Chaldeans. For I will set My eyes on them for good, and I will bring them back to this land; I will build them and not pull them down, and I will plant them and not pluck them up." (Jer. 24:5–6)

God was sending his people into captivity for their own good. His love for them required Him to save them from the sinfulness where they currently lived. Jeremiah's work was paying off. His patient continuance of offering hope and love to those who would listen was going to finally bear fruit.

Many people think God in the Old Testament is harsh and all judgment. Yet here is an example of His love and mercy for His people. God has not changed. He is the same God in the New Testament. His love and mercy are evident in both Testaments if we look for it. God's love is also shown in Jeremiah 26:1–3:

> In the beginning of the reign of Jehoiakim the son of Josiah, king of Judah, this word came from the LORD, saying, "Thus says the LORD: 'Stand in the court of the LORD's house, and speak to all the cities of Judah, which come to worship in the LORD's house, all the words that I command you to speak to them. Do not diminish a word. Perhaps everyone will listen and turn from his evil way, that I may relent concerning the calamity which I purpose to bring on them because of the evil of their doings.'"

We may miss the evidence of God's love because the people reacted with evil intent in verses 7–8:

> So the priests and the prophets and all the people heard Jeremiah speaking these words in the house of the LORD. Now it happened, when Jeremiah had made an end of speaking all that the LORD had commanded him to speak to all the people, that the priests and the prophets and all the people seized him, saying, "You will surely die!"

Jeremiah continued to speak to the people as God directed. As a result, he was imprisoned. Jerusalem was under siege, as Jeremiah had prophesied:

> And Jeremiah the prophet was shut up in the court of the prison, which was in the king of

> Judah's house. For Zedekiah king of Judah had shut him up, saying, "Why do you prophesy and say, 'Thus says the LORD: Behold, I will give this city into the hand of the king of Babylon, and he shall take it.'" (Jer. 32:2–3)

God continued to offer opportunities for His people to hear His warnings and repent:

> Take a scroll of a book and write on it all the words that I have spoken to you against Israel, against Judah, and against all the nations, from the day I spoke to you, from the days of Josiah even to this day. It may be that the house of Judah will hear all the adversities which I purpose to bring upon them, that everyone may turn from his evil way, that I may forgive their iniquity and their sin. (Jer. 36:2–3)

Jeremiah, though in prison, dictated the scroll. Baruch wrote it and then read it in the temple. The princes then had Baruch read it to them (this was his second reading of the entire scroll). They were struck with fear. They took Baruch to the king. Baruch read the scroll to the king (his third reading of the entire scroll). As Baruch read, the king cut the read portions off the scroll and dropped them in the fire. The entire scroll was destroyed.

Jeremiah re-dictated the entire scroll, with more prophesies, which is what we read today in the book of Jeremiah. That is patience. Jeremiah and Baruch had to re-do all the work they had done. This would have been a lengthy process. Yet they obeyed the Lord and loved the people enough to not quit or give up, despite how bad things looked. God had not given up on His people. Jeremiah could not give up on them either.

Patience is not an easy weapon to wield. It has great power to overcome the enemy but requires a determination on the part of the soldier using it. Luke 8:15 says, "But the ones that fell on the good ground are those who, having heard the word with a noble and good heart, keep it and bear fruit with patience." Jeremiah's fruit, long-term, was at least twofold:

1. The lives of those who heard his words whom God carried off for their own good into captivity. These would be the future of the nation. Jeremiah preserved the nation of Israel by patiently obeying the Lord for over forty years.
2. The Book of Jeremiah, which is still being read and studied today. Written from approximately 630–580 BC, it has survived for over 2,500 years. That is marvelous fruit. Patience bears long term fruit.

Luke 21:19 records Jesus as saying, "By your patience possess your souls." The context is much like what Jeremiah went through:

> For I will give you a mouth and wisdom which all your adversaries will not be able to contradict or resist. You will be betrayed even by parents and brothers, relatives and friends; and they will put some of you to death. And you will be hated by all for My name's sake. But not a hair of your head shall be lost. By your patience possess your souls. (Luke 21:15–19)

Jesus was talking to his disciples as well as the people who were in the temple in Jerusalem. Therefore, we can know that He is also speaking these words to us, as His believers, today. Patience helps us to be victorious over hard times.

Trials in our lives help us develop patience. It is actually a good thing to pray for patience. It is not the coward's way, but it is good for our souls. We can only possess (own) our souls through patience. "Souls" in Luke 21:19 refers to our lives, not our spirit. Patience gives us life. Stress, worry, or fear shortens our life span because they cause wear and tear on our bodies. Patience defeats each of those weapons of the enemy against our souls. Simply put, we win if we don't give up.

Romans 8:25 says, "But if we hope for what we do not see, we eagerly wait for it with perseverance." Perseverance is patience. We patiently wait for God's promises to come true in our lives. We know God cannot lie. His word is powerful and creates as soon as He says it, so we know we can have it. We patiently and cheerfully wait for it.

God is patient with us, according to Romans 15:5: "Now may the God of patience and comfort grant you to be like-minded toward one another, according to Christ Jesus." God has patience with our frailty. He expects us to be "like-minded" and have patience toward others. We are to be of the same mindset (patient) as Christ Jesus.

The Scriptures were written for our learning: "That we through the patience and comfort of the Scriptures might have hope" (Rom. 15:4). The Scriptures are patient in that they continually teach us, layer upon layer, as we read them. New truths are revealed to us as we grow in our knowledge and relationship with God.

The Scriptures are alive. What are the Scriptures? The Word of God. John 1:1–2 says, "In the beginning was the Word, and the Word was with God, and the Word was God. He was in the beginning with God." Jesus is the Word of God, according to 1 John 1:1–2 and 1 John 5:7:

> That which was from the beginning, which we have heard, which we have seen with our eyes, which we have looked upon, and our hands have handled, concerning the Word of life—the life was manifested, and we have seen, and bear witness, and declare to you that eternal life which was with the Father and was manifested to us...
> For there are three that bear witness in heaven: the Father, the Word, and the Holy Spirit; and these three are one.

The Scriptures are a manifestation of Jesus for us. They are alive. First Peter 1:23 and 25 says, "The word of God which lives and abides forever…but the word of the LORD endures forever." The Word is Jesus. The Word is alive eternally since Jesus is eternally alive, and God is life. Jesus is patient with us; the Scriptures are patient with us. We are to be like Jesus, which means we are to be patient also.

This is not an easy thing, but Paul prayed for us to have patience in Colossians 1:9–11:

> For this reason we also…do not cease to pray for you, and to ask that you may be filled with the knowledge of His will in all wisdom and spiritual understanding;…being fruitful in every good work and increasing in the knowledge of God; strengthened with all might, according to His glorious power, for all patience and longsuffering with joy.

We know since Paul prayed this prayer, that God would answer it. First John 5:14–15 says, "Now this is the confidence that we have in Him, that if we ask anything according to His will, He hears us. And if we know that He hears us, whatever we ask, we know that we have the petitions that we have asked of Him." Paul's prayer for the Colossians, and for us, must be God's will since it is recorded in Scripture. So we really have no excuse. We are to be patient. It is not optional. We have been strengthened in all power according to the might of His glory to be patient and forbearing in everything with joy.

In the future, patience is one of two weapons that will help believers overcome the beast that makes war with the saints and blasphemes God, His Name, and His Tabernacle. Believers will not pay homage to him:

> All who dwell on the earth will worship him, whose names have not been written in the Book of Life of the Lamb slain from the foundation of the world. If anyone has an ear, let him

hear. He who leads into captivity shall go into captivity; he who kills with the sword must be killed with the sword. Here is the patience and the faith of the saints. (Rev. 13:8–10)

Much like in Jeremiah's time, God in His mercy may in the future send His people into captivity to preserve them. Even if He does not, the situation (personal and worldwide) will certainly look extremely bleak at times. Believers are to not look at the immediate short-term situation, but with patience, we are to look to the hope that is promised to us all. We will overcome by constancy of our faith and continuance of our waiting in patience for God's will to be worked in our lives.

We will not be deceived by the miracles the beast will be able to do because we know the truth of Scripture. Believers will not panic because God has forewarned us this would happen, so we can know we are still in God's will. His promise to never leave us nor forsake us is still in effect. His eye is still on every one of His children. We will not be abandoned. We can be patient, having faith, hope, and joy that our Redeemer is with us, no matter what it looks like.

10

EIGHTH WEAPON: COVENANT OF SALT

Salt.

Not pepper.

Salt. We have a very important weapon on our belt of truth—the covenant of salt.

Second Chronicles 13:5 says, "Should you not know that the LORD God of Israel gave the dominion over Israel to David forever, to him and his sons, by a covenant of salt?" There is a covenant of salt that God has with His believers. Leviticus 2:13 talks about this covenant: "And every offering of your grain offering you shall season with salt; you shall not allow the salt of the covenant of your God to be lacking from your grain offering. With all your offerings you shall offer salt." Numbers 18:19 also talks about this covenant: "All the heave offerings of the holy things, which the children of Israel offer to the LORD, I have given to you and your sons and daughters with you as an ordinance forever; it is a covenant of salt forever before the LORD with you and your descendants with you." The priests were allowed to eat most of the offerings brought by the people to the Lord. Some were to be eaten in a most holy place; some were to be eaten any place. Some were only for the priests; some were also for their families to eat. When eaten, all these offerings were, in essence, eaten with God. They "had salt between them," and while a Spirit, God was with them.

Samuel, as recorded in 1 Samuel 16, anointed David as the future king over Israel. This was done, according to 2 Chronicles 13:5, as a covenant of salt. In 1 Samuel 16, God instructed Samuel to take a heifer with him to sacrifice to the Lord and invite Jesse and his sons to the sacrifice. Jesse left the youngest son, David, out in the field with the sheep. Samuel would not sit down to eat until David was there. While Scripture does not record that they actually ate the sacrifice, it is implied that Samuel offered the heifer as a sacrifice. The elders of Bethlehem, as well as Jesse and all his sons ate with Samuel after anointing David with his horn of oil. This was the covenant of salt. Samuel was representative of God. They sat down and had a celebratory meal together, marking the occasion of David's anointing.

The covenant of salt mentioned in all the above verses is never actually defined in Scriptures. To understand the concepts of the covenant of salt, we will start with salt itself. The root word behind the word *salt* in Hebrew means properly to be rubbed to pieces, and to disappear as dust. There are two meanings of the root: to season with salt internally, or to season with salt externally by rubbing with salt. Salt itself in Hebrew implies a powder easily pulverized and dissolved.

Salt is a mineral made up of two elements: sodium and chlorine. Sodium never exists by itself in nature. It is an alkali metal so unstable that it bursts into flames when exposed to water. Chlorine is a lethal gas. However, when these two elements are combined in an ionic bond in proper proportions, they turn into a strongly held together life-giving agent.

Salt is essential to life. Our bodies need it for muscle contraction and for nerve impulses that are the body's communication network. Salt regulates the exchange of water between cells and surrounding fluids. It helps carry food in and waste out of every cell in our body. Without salt, our body would go into convulsions, paralysis, and death. If a blood cell is put into a salt-free solution, it will burst.

Looking at this information, we can make the analogy that we are extremely unstable when living life without God. Approaching God without the covering atonement of Yeshua's blood, we would disappear as dust due to our sinful nature and God's power and holiness. Even David said in Psalm 8:4, "What is man that You are mindful of him, and the son of man that You visit him?" Man was formed from the dust of the Earth according to Genesis 2:7. Yet in God's glorious mercy and loving generosity, when we are combined together with Him through faith, such a strong bond occurs that He acknowledges it with His promise to never leave us or forsake us.

Without God, we cannot have eternal life. Yeshua is the only door into a relationship with God and eternal life. Yeshua is the Word itself, which is our bread. The Word goes into us, giving us eternal life, and the Word draws the waste (our sinfulness) out of us.

Salt is a preservative. It draws moisture out of bacteria, which kills it. Germs cannot live in salt. The Latin meaning of preservative means "to guard beforehand." Protect means "to cover in front" in Latin. Just as God is our shield, He covers us in front and guards us before hand from attacks of the enemy. Psalm 127:1 declares, "Unless the LORD builds the house, they labor in vain who build it: unless the LORD guards the city, the watchman stays awake in vain." God is our protection. Our efforts are feeble at best and often futile.

In ancient times, salt was used to seal a truce between enemies, or to seal a bond of loyalty between friends. Treaties or friendships were formalized and sealed when both parties partook of salt together. These covenants were of loyalty and truthfulness, even unto death. They were not entered into casually. The phrase "There is salt between us" is still used today among some Eastern people, recognizing this covenant that forms when sitting at a table together, eating together. Abraham had salt between him and God. In Genesis 14:18, Abraham shared bread and wine with the king of Salem, Melchizedek. Melchizedek was a pre-incarnate appearance of Jesus (see Hebrews 5:6 and Hebrews 6:19–7:3). Abraham also had salt between him and God in Genesis 18. This concept of bread and wine is also what we do in communion whenever we have it. We are doing it in remembrance of the Passover meal with Jesus. We are partaking by faith of the covenants offered to us by God. We are saying, "There is salt between us."

We can see this covenant of salt, even though it is not specifically mentioned, in how King David treated Mephibosheth, the son of Jonathan and grandson of Saul.

Long before he became king of Israel, David made a covenant of salt with Jonathan, Saul's son, since they ate together daily when David played the harp to calm and soothe Saul. David and Jonathan had made a covenant as referenced in 1 Samuel 18:3. When David had to inform Jonathan that Saul intended to kill David, he invoked that covenant as recorded in 1 Samuel 20:8: "Therefore you shall deal kindly with your servant, for you have brought your servant into a covenant of the LORD with you."

Once Jonathan discovered the murder threat against David was real, he met David in a field to say goodbye. There, he reminded David of their covenant and made David promise to care for his family. First Samuel 20:14–15 records what Jonathan said:

> "And you shall not only show me the kindness of the LORD while I still live, that I may not die; but you shall not cut off your kindness from my house forever, no, not when the LORD has cut off every one of the enemies of David from the face of the earth." So Jonathan made a covenant with the house of David.

He again reminded David of this covenant at their final goodbye in 1 Samuel 20:42: "Go in peace, since we have both sworn in the name of the LORD, saying, 'May the LORD be between you and me, and between your descendants and my descendants, forever.'"

David remembered this covenant when he became king. Second Samuel 9:1 says David asked, "Is there still anyone who is left of the house of Saul, that I may show him kindness for Jonathan's sake?" Second Samuel 4:4 mentions Jonathan's son: "Jonathan, Saul's son, had a son who was lame in his feet. He was five years old when the news about Saul and Jonathan came from Jezreel; and his nurse took him up and fled. And it happened, as she made haste to flee, that he fell and became lame. His name was Mephibosheth." Upon hearing that Saul and Jonathan were both killed, the nurse grabbed Jonathan's son, five-year-old Mephibosheth, to flee. It was very common for the new king to kill all remaining family members of the old king to ensure there would be no contestants for the throne. That was why the nurse grabbed the boy and was intending to flee into hiding. In her haste, the boy fell and became lame for the rest of his life.

King David sent for Mephibosheth. Second Samuel 9:6–7 says,

> Now when Mephibosheth the son of Jonathan, the son of Saul, had come to David, he fell on his face and prostrated himself. Then David said, "Mephibosheth?" And he answered, "Here is your servant!" So David said to him, "Do not fear, for I will surely show you kindness for Jonathan your father's sake, and will restore to you all the land of Saul your grandfather; and you shall eat bread at my table continually."

David invited Mephibosheth to live with him, eat at the king's table at David's expense, and be taken care of by David. Notice that David said he would show this kindness for Jonathan's sake—for the sake of the covenant they had made. In essence, David was continuing that covenant, plus extending a covenant of salt to Mephibosheth for provision, protection, and relationship.

Mephibosheth had a decision to make at that moment. Being crippled or lame from the age of five, every time he wanted to walk, to run as a child and play like others, to move from one spot to another, he was reminded that he was lame because of David. David did not cause the nurse to flee—fear did. That nurse probably told Mephibosheth, if he did not remember himself, that she was fleeing after hearing of Mephibosheth's father's and grandfather's deaths. She was fleeing out of fear of being killed by David to seal his possession of the throne of Israel. Mephibosheth could have developed bitterness against David. He could have been bitter about the lameness he experienced. He could have been bitter about the fact he was not king since he was the grandson of Saul.

Mephibosheth was faced with the choice of continuing to live in apparent poverty and pity, or he could choose the offer of living with the king, like royalty. The unspoken covenant of salt being offered to him was a covenant based on trust. Could Mephibosheth lay aside his old thought patterns, bitterness, unforgiveness, or whatever was in his heart regarding David? Could he trust this king to take care of him? Did he want to? Staying in old patterns is comfortable because it is known. While the new may be much better, it is still unknown and therefore frightening. Bitterness, being nursed over years, can be a pretty comfortable place to live emotionally. It is not right nor is it fun, but it is comfortable because it is known.

Mephibosheth's answer was an indirect one: "What is your servant, that you should look upon such a dead dog as I?" (2 Sam. 9:8) David didn't answer that question directly, but he did immediately give a decree that began to prove to Mephibosheth that the king was trustworthy and meant what he offered. He ordered all of Saul's lands be given to Mephibosheth, and the harvest from those lands to be for Mephibosheth's benefit.

Instead of answering Mephibosheth's question of "why me?" with verbal statements of good intention, David answered with actions that proved his intentions. David showed by these decrees that he was trustworthy and that Mephibosheth could indeed enter into relationship with David in David's house, in David's care, and at David's table. The covenant of salt was extended to Mephibosheth for the sake of the covenant with Jonathan, but also for Mephibosheth's sake as well.

Mephibosheth accepted David's offer and learned that the value of the covenant of salt was in relationship and trust. He ultimately and willingly gave up his inheritance and wealth to maintain relationship with David. This is a picture of our relationship with God, and the covenant of salt He offers to each of us. He provides us with provision, protection, and relationship in exchange for our trust of Him. Mephibosheth was not required to bring anything into the relationship except his trust and his presence at the king's table. He received benefits way beyond his meager ability to offer anything in exchange. That's the same with us—God gives us benefits merely for trusting Him and spending time with Him in relationship. We have nothing to offer Him in exchange except our trust, our presence, and our love. Mephibosheth offered his love when he declared he didn't care about his inheritance, he only wanted relationship with David (see 2 Samuel 19:29–30).

Every time we say grace before we eat a meal, we are invoking the covenant of salt God offers us. We, in essence, invite Him to the table with us as we acknowledge His provision of our food. Never underestimate the power of saying grace. I have a friend who was born in Africa. Her family was not happy when she became a Christian and abandoned the family's gods. They were convinced she was crazy to believe in an invisible God who loved her. One day, she told me, she was visiting her family and they gave her a soft drink to drink. She paused and said grace before drinking the soda pop. As she finished saying grace, the glass exploded in front of her. The family confessed that they had poisoned the drink since they had decided she would be better off dead in their opinion than Christian. God exploded the glass so she wouldn't drink the poison. This also proved to her family that her God was real and powerful enough to protect her. They eventually all came to faith in Jesus too.

To further understand the meaning of the covenant of salt, we can learn more by understanding what salt does. Salt's effects are why the covenant of salt is such a powerful weapon of warfare for believers. First of all, let's go back to the Hebrew meaning for *salt*, which is to be rubbed to pieces, to dissolve like dust. When we are in relationship with God, we are to allow God to rub the rough edges off of us, to polish us so we are more like Jesus. We are to decrease and allow Jesus to increase inside us, so we are to dissolve like dust, in a way.

Salt also retards the spread of decay. As mentioned, salt draws moisture out of bacteria, which then kills the bacteria. Salt provides warmth and thus it is used to melt ice. Salt also is used to soften water by drawing the hard minerals out. God retards and stops the spread of decay from sin in our lives once we accept Jesus as our Savior. God warms our hearts toward Him so we can accept Yeshua. God is capable of "melting" the hardest of hearts and giving His grace to the worst of sinners so they desire to say "yes" to Jesus as their personal Savior. So a covenant of salt with God stops and retards the spread of decay in a believer's life. It melts the hardness out of our hearts, heads, and spirits to allow less of us and more of Jesus to shine through. This covenant also gives us eternal life, the warmth of life eternally. The covenant of salt gives us life. Salt is necessary for life, just as the covenant of salt with God is necessary for eternal life and for the "more abundantly" life Jesus came to give us while here on Earth (John 10:10).

As a weapon on our belt, we can use the covenant of salt to protect our own family and also for lifestyle evangelism with the unbelievers. As a protection for our own families, it has been proven in over twenty years of studies that children who eat regularly with their parents succeed better emotionally, socially, and academically when compared to children in families that do not eat together. My granddaughter knows, and some of my own children knew, children who never eat with their family at a table together. In some cases, the parents are too busy for everyone to even be in the same place at the same time to sit down and eat. In some cases, they may all be in the same house, but they all get their plate of food and go to different rooms to watch individual television shows rather than sit and talk together. The dinner table is a great place to keep in touch with each member's life, to teach the children life lessons from God's word as they come up naturally over the course of time, and to discuss current events with them so they are prepared to understand God's word and how it applies to every aspect of their lives when they grow up. Just by taking the time to eat together, parents can instill a strong sense of purity and integrity in their children over time.

As a preservative, the covenant of salt means we can pray for our families and protect them and guard them through prayers to the One who can do what we cannot. Sodium and chloride ions combine into salt and form almost perfect cubes. When large salt cubes are broken apart, the smaller ones are also formed in almost perfect cubes. When we take the time to "have salt between us" in relationships, we can replicate ourselves. Parents can instill Christian values into their children; discipleship can occur wherein the believer replicates him or herself. The presence of salt, and the presence of believers regularly in the life of vulnerable children or new believers, enables them to resist defilement and spoiling (decay through sin). It can also arrest or stop what is already in progress, such as bad behavior, ungodly behavior, or wrong thought patterns and attitudes.

Salt also creates thirst, so the covenant of salt is a powerful weapon for believers to use in evangelism. Our family life is often a lifestyle evangelism we are unaware of. As our children continuously grow in Christ because we recognize teachable moments while eating and talking the day over as a family, the parents can refer the events of their lives back to Scriptures. Our behavior can create a thirst in the unbeliever for what we have. Our love and relationships with each other also create that thirst. One of my granddaughter's friends stated that her family never eats together. She thought it was weird that my granddaughter's family did, yet she stayed over for dinner many times each week. When my children were growing up, their friends usually hung out at our house too and stayed for meals. Children are drawn to that love and relationship that exists when the family takes and makes the time to gather together at each meal.

Salt is a seasoning. It brings out the flavor of food. We can use the covenant of salt—mealtime—to speak words of life into others, to bring out the real person God created and to bring out the real talents/gifts God placed in each person. We spend enough time with them, eating with them, to know them well enough to help them succeed. We can speak their destiny into them and help them with their talents to be who God created them to be.

Salt also requires distribution. To be most effective, salt should be spread evenly. All the salt clumped in one spot on the food leaves the rest more bland and one bad, very salty mouthful. We are to have relationships with unbelievers so we can create a thirst in them for the gospel. We are to know them well enough to speak words of encouragement, life, and love into their lives.

As an example, I joined a women's golf league to meet new women and make new friends. Many of the women, to my surprise, had the bad habit of using foul language. I never said a word, although I was initially surprised by the language choice. I realized that most of my friends were fellow believers, and I just was no longer around people who swore or used bad words. A few months later, I was golfing with one of the women whom I had met. She swore, and then apologized to me about it. I had never said anything, but I guess she felt the conviction of God. I commented that my children had started to pick up swear words from fellow students in school. I stopped them every time they said a swear word, and told them there were plenty of words in the English language for them to find a more appropriate way to describe what they were trying to express. Swearing is just a bad habit. In this way, I was able to stop the decay of my children's language. Through referring back to how I dealt with my children regarding the habit of swearing, I was able to not condemn her but encourage her to start overcoming a habit she realized she needed to overcome.

Salt is even used in incense offerings. Exodus 30:34–35 says, "And the Lord said to Moses: 'Take sweet spices…and pure frankincense with these sweet spices; there shall be equal amounts of each. You shall make of these an incense, a compound according to the art of the perfumer, salted, pure, and holy.'" We are to be the sweet fragrance of Christ to God. We are the fragrance of life to unbelievers, according to 2 Corinthians 2:15–16. We offer our own lives to God and thus we are a sweet aroma to Him—salted, pure, and holy. Jesus also tells us in Mark 9:50 to "have salt in yourselves, and have peace with one another."

The concept of salt's importance in relationships is again pointed out to believers in Colossians 4:6. We are reminded, "Let your speech always be with grace, seasoned with salt, that you may know how you ought to answer each one." We are to create thirst in others for more of God in their own lives. We are to preserve, protect, prevent decay, create warmth, and take away hardness. These are all things that salt does.

Salt also promotes cleanliness. Salt is necessary to make soda ash, which is used to make soap. Our words are to always be with grace, seasoned with salt. We have to be full of God's love and Spirit to have the grace of God flow in our words. Only through relationship with the living Father can we know how we are to answer each other. Words spoken without filtering them through Christ can hurt, rather than give life. A hard correction, done in love and with Christ as our filter, can be received and bring life, halt decay, and soften hardness.

The sin offerings described in Ezekiel 43:19–26 were to be salted. Verse 24 says, "When you offer them before the LORD, the priests shall throw salt on them, and they will offer them up as a burnt offering to the LORD." Sin offerings require salt on them. Jesus said believers are salt, in Matthew 5:13: "You are the salt of the earth; but if the salt loses its flavor, how shall it be seasoned? It is then good for nothing but to be thrown out and trampled underfoot by men." We are to retain our saltiness. This means we are to stay in close relationship with God not only for our own benefit, but also for the benefit of the world. If we are the salt of the Earth, we throw our words of grace, seasoned with salt, on the ears of others. They can then offer their sins up to God for forgiveness because we, as believers who are all priests before God, have thrown salt on them.

In another example of the power of salt to cleanse and heal, 2 Kings 2:19–21 records how Elisha healed bad water with salt:

> Then the men of the city said to Elisha, "Please notice, the situation of this city is pleasant…but the water is bad, and the ground barren." And he said, "Bring me a new bowl, and put salt in it." So they brought it to him. Then he went out to the source of the water, and cast in the salt there, and said, "Thus says the LORD: 'I have healed this water; from it there shall be no more death or barrenness.'"

The salt poured on the source of bad water healed the water and cleansed the land of barrenness.

We are to be that salt to the world around us. We are to allow God to spread us out, distributing us where He desires to salt the unclean and make it clean through Christ. God does all the cleaning, warming, cleansing, etc. We are just the agent; He is the chemical reaction itself doing the work He desires.

Our ability to be used so successfully by God is the result of our covenant of salt with Him. Our covenant of salt is only because of our trust in God. He alone can keep us, protect us, preserve us, and use us to bring cleansing, thirst, warmth, softness, and life to others. These are all reasons why this is such a powerful weapon of warfare on our belt of truth. These are reasons why we can be people of faith, hope, and joy.

11

Ninth Weapon: The Blood of Jesus

I had the privilege of hearing Betty Malz, a Christian speaker and author who had a death experience, speak many years ago. She told a story that has stayed with me all these years. She and her husband were traveling for ministry. They had young children whom they left at home, in the care of grandparents while they were on this particular trip. She recalled that she was woken up during the night with an urgent pressure to pray for their children. She discovered that her husband was also up, having just woken up with the same pressure. They prayed protection over their children, and over the land where the children were staying. She told us that she and her husband prayed the blood of Jesus over the property lines during that night's intercession. I gathered from her story that the property was not just a city-size bit of grass around the house. It was larger, more like what could be considered a small ranch as I recall.

After they prayed together, Betty and her husband were released to go back to sleep. The next opportunity they could, they talked with the grandparents to see how the children were doing, but did not tell him they were up praying during the night. The grandfather said the children were fine. He then commented that he decided to check the property line on the morning after Betty and her husband had prayed. Every few feet, he found a dead fox right on the property line. Seeing so many of them was unusual, so he took a few of them to the veterinarian for examination. It turns out that every dead fox was rabid. Every one of them had rabies. Betty's point to her story was that she and her husband had applied the blood of Jesus to their property lines as part of their prayers of protection over their family. With the number of rabid foxes found all along their property line, the children would have had high chances of getting bit by at least one fox, if not many more. Each fox died at the line of the blood— the property line—and could not cross it to harm the family. Her point—the blood of Jesus is powerful. The enemy cannot cross the blood line when we pray it.

For a period of time, I was awakened each night, at the same time every night, with an urgency to pray protection over my house and family too. This went on for a long while. I can't remember if it was months, or a year, or more. I just remember it was a season. I looked out a front window, keeping all the lights off in the house, and saw an old car parked right in front of our house. One night I even saw a man walking on the street curb of our property. The Lord woke me at the same time every single night to pray. I routinely pray the blood of Jesus over each family member and over all aspects of our lives. However, in this time period, the intensity of warfare had increased dramatically.

I was fighting something evil, and fear was waging its war against me as part of that. I didn't even want to walk to the kitchen (also at the front of the house) to get my morning coffee because fear was so intense. I finally moved the coffee pot onto my side of the bathroom sink at the back of the house, so I could have my coffee and prayer time with Father God as usual. That worked. By the time I got done with my morning prayers, I was no longer battling fear. The nightly prayer time lasted about an hour every night. I knew the car pulled away, with its lights still off because I could feel the difference when I didn't actually watch it pull away. Soon after that, I felt the need to pray recede, and I could go back to sleep easily. For the record, I was never tired from the lack of sleep every night.

I knew whoever was in that car could not walk on our grass or our property because the blood of Jesus was drawn around it in prayer. I am thankful for the large angels someone told me they saw in every room of my house that faces the street. She told me they are posted there permanently to keep evil out. I am so grateful for the power of the blood of Jesus and the fact we can use this weapon when fighting the enemy.

Why the Blood of Jesus Works

Jesus shed His blood at the cross for us. By doing so, He became our mediator with the Father: "And for this reason He is the Mediator of the new covenant, by means of death, for the redemption of the transgressions under the first covenant, that those who are called may receive the promise of the eternal inheritance" (Heb. 9:15). Galatians 1:3–4 reiterates this: "Grace to you and peace from God the Father and our Lord Jesus Christ, who gave Himself for our sins, that He might deliver us from this present evil age, according to the will of our God and Father." First Timothy 2:5–6 also says this, "For there is one God and one Mediator between God and men, the Man Christ Jesus, who gave Himself a ransom for all." Man always needed a mediator after the fall in the Garden of Eden. Job cries out for such a mediator in Job 16:21: "Oh, that one might plead for a man with God, as a man pleads for his neighbor!"

As our mediator, Christ intercedes for us continually. Romans 8:34 says, "Who is he who condemns? It is Christ who died, and furthermore is also risen, who is even at the right hand of God, who also makes intercession for us." Hebrews 7:25–26 also says of Jesus: "Therefore He is also able to save to the uttermost those who come to God through Him, since He always lives to make intercession for them. For such a High Priest was fitting for us, who is holy, harmless, undefiled, separate from sinners, and has become higher than the heavens."

The only reason Christ can be our mediator in heaven is because He is both God and man. First Samuel 2:25 points out: "If one man sins against another, God will judge him. But if a man sins against the LORD, who will intercede for him?" The priests could mediate some sins for the Israelites under the original covenant, but not all. They were totally incapable of dealing with the overall sin nature of mankind. They played a limited role in mediation. Philippians 2:6–9 says this about Jesus:

> Who, being in the form of God, did not consider it robbery to be equal with God, but made Himself of no reputation, taking the form of a bond-servant, and coming in the likeness of men. And being found in appearance as a man, He humbled Himself and became obedient to the point of death, even the death of the cross. Therefore God also has highly exalted Him and given Him the name which is above every name.

Hebrews 2:14 also talks about Jesus partaking of flesh and blood just like all the children: "Inasmuch then as the children have partaken of flesh and blood, He Himself likewise shared in the same, that through death He might destroy him who had the power of death, that is, the devil."

Jesus was sinless, but became our sin bearer. Instead of symbolically cleansing us from defilement, the Lord cleansed us from actual sin. As our high priest, Jesus is holy, harmless, undefiled, separate from sinners but nevertheless touched with the feeling of our infirmities and weaknesses (Heb. 4:15). Thus, we can come boldly to Him today to obtain grace and mercy, a relationship with the living, one true God, and all that such a relationship provides for us. The blood of Jesus is the most powerful weapon of warfare we have. Without the shed blood of Jesus, none of us could be redeemed from the clutches of sin that so easily beset us, nor could we be redeemed from the kingdom of darkness into the kingdom of light.

The shed blood of Jesus gives us the confidence to enter the Holy of Holies, God's throne room. It also gives us the confidence to reach the lost. Acts 4:13 shows the boldness we are to have: "Now when they saw the boldness of Peter and John, and perceived that they were uneducated and untrained men, they marveled. And they realized that they had been with Jesus." Acts 4:29–31 shows that boldness again:

> "Now, Lord, look on their threats, and grant to Your servants that with all boldness they may speak Your word, by stretching out Your hand to heal, and that signs and wonders may be done through the name of Your holy Servant Jesus." And when they had prayed, the place where they were assembled together was shaken; and they were all filled with the Holy Spirit, and they spoke the word of God with boldness.

The disciples were uneducated. We do not need a degree in theology to be effective witnesses to the lost. Holy Spirit helped the disciples speak the words of God. Satan will tell us the unbelievers we encounter may ask some question we won't be able to answer if we start to tell them about Jesus. We then think we don't know the answer to that "what if" question. Therefore, we don't speak out at all. We have given in to the enemy's tactic of fear. Proverbs 28:1 says, "The wicked flee when no one pursues, but the righteous are bold as a lion." It is the blood of Jesus that gives His followers the boldness needed to reach the lost. "Through Him we have received grace and apostleship for obedience to the faith among all nations for His name" (Rom. 1:5).

Classical mythology believed that a golden fluid, called ichor, and an ethereal fluid of blood and water flowed in the veins of the gods. When the Roman soldier pierced Jesus's side and a gush of blood and water poured out, that was partially why he cried, "Truly this was the Son of God!" Jesus is the Word and what flows in His veins cleanses us. That "water" from His blood washes us clean. Isaiah 12:3 declares, "Therefore with joy you will draw water from the wells of salvation." Ezekiel 36:25 records God saying, "Then I will sprinkle clean water on you, and you shall be clean; I will cleanse you from all your filthiness and from all your idols." Jesus, Himself, hints of this cleansing in John 4:10: "Jesus answered and said to her, 'If you knew the gift of God, and who it is who says to you, 'Give Me a drink,' You would have asked Him, and He would have given you living water." Ephesians 5:26 says that Jesus sanctifies and cleanses the church (all believers) with the washing of water by the word.

The Lord is also light, as Psalm 27:1 reiterates: "The LORD is my light and my salvation; whom shall I fear?" Isaiah 9:2 is talking about Jesus when it says: "The people who walked in darkness have seen a great light; those who dwell in the land of the shadow of death, upon them a light has shined." Isaiah 42:6 refers to Jesus as a light to the Gentiles. In the New Testament, John 1:4 and 9 says of Jesus: "In Him was life, and the life was the light of men... That was the true Light which gives light to every man coming into the world."

Leviticus 17:11 says that life is in the blood: "For the life of the flesh is in the blood...for it is the blood that makes atonement for the soul." Jesus is light, He is the Word, He is eternally alive. His blood alone makes atonement for all the souls of all the believers through all the centuries. Adam was originally not created to die. God formed Adam out of the dust of the Earth, then breathed into him the breath of life, according to Genesis 2:7, and man became a living soul. The breath of God put something in Adam that made him alive. That breath had to be the blood since the life is in the blood.

A French scientist, Gaston Naessens, named tiny blood particles "somatids." These blood particles were invisible until the invention of the light microscope. Scientists have since found somatids to be indestructible, unaffected by extreme high temperatures, extremely toxic chemicals, or even nuclear radiation. Dried blood, when reconstituted, will show life activity in the somatids. This is proof of what Scripture says: life is in the blood. This is why the blood of Jesus works—it alone has the cleansing life and light we need to live in proper relationship with God. Jesus alone is the only qualified priest to offer this sacrifice for us.

How the Blood of Jesus Works

All men are related by the blood of Adam—sinful, polluted, dead in sin. Acts 17:26 says, "And He has made from one blood every nation of men to dwell on all the face of the earth, and has determined their preappointed times and the boundaries of their dwellings." We are all descendants of Adam. Adam sinned and received the sentence of eventual physical death. Because of this, all men die. Again, since the life is in the blood, and the wages of sin is death, sin had to have affected Adam's blood.

God knows all things. He is the great I AM, which means He is present before the creation of the world, He is present when Adam sinned, and He is present with the full plan of salvation before the foundations of the world. That full plan of salvation required a sinless sacrifice to atone for all sins for all who chose to believe or "faith" Jesus. We know Jesus was sinless because of 2 Corinthians 5:21: "For He made Him who knew no sin to be sin for us, that we might become the righteousness of God in Him."

When God created Eve, He designed her body to give birth with the future need for a sinless man in mind. An unborn baby's blood is not derived from the mother. It is actually produced within the body of the unborn baby inside the mother's womb. The blood appears only after the sperm has entered the ovum and the baby begins to develop in the mother's womb. To say it again, the blood of the unborn baby only appears after the sperm has fertilized the egg. In simple words, the unborn baby's blood comes from the father, not the mother. The mother provides the baby with nutrition needed for development inside the womb, but not her blood. All the blood that forms in the baby is formed in the embryo itself. From the time of conception to the time of birth, no blood ever passes between mother and baby.

The placenta forms the link between mother and child. All nutrition and even antibodies are passed from mother to the baby thru the placenta. Waste products from the child are passed back to the mother through the placenta. No blood is exchanged. All the blood within the baby was formed within the baby. This is why the virgin birth is such an important issue in the doctrines of our faith.

Jesus's blood is divine. He was conceived by Holy Spirit overshadowing the virgin Mary (Matt. 1:18–20, 22–23). His blood, therefore, was sinless since His Father is sinless. Jesus's blood is innocent blood. Matthew 27:4 records Judas saying, "I have sinned by betraying innocent blood." Jesus even said He was innocent in John 14:30, just before his arrest: "I will no longer talk much with you, for the ruler of this world is coming, and he has nothing in Me."

Also, because the blood of Jesus is sinless, it is incorruptible. Remember, the wages of sin is death. Jesus is eternal. Without sin, He was without death, or corruption/decay. First Peter 1:18–19 says, "Knowing that you were not redeemed with corruptible things, like silver or gold, from your aimless conduct received by tradition from your fathers, but with the precious blood of Christ, as of a lamb without blemish and without spot."

This should amaze you and fill you with hope, joy, and faith! If God could design such an intricate body knowing that at the right moment a few thousand years after Eve that He could bring forth a baby from a virgin, He certainly is not caught unaware of whatever problem you are facing today. He went through such intricate and incredible creation to provide the needed atonement for sinful mankind, it should prove to us that He will take care of us in every aspect of our needs too.

Jesus took the sin of others upon Himself and died the death each believer deserves. He chose to give up His life—He was not killed. Matthew 27:50 says, "And Jesus cried out again with a loud voice, and yielded up His spirit." See also John 19:30. The Greek word for *yielded* (*Strong's* #863) means to send forth, lay aside, leave, send or put away, remit, yield up. All these indicate it is an active action—a choice. Jesus's life was not taken from Him. He gave it to His Father. He willingly died.

Soon after death, decay sets in, and it begins in the blood. Yet Psalm 49:9 declares that the Messiah will not decay. "That he should continue to live eternally, and not see the Pit." Psalm 16:10 also prophesied this: "For you will not leave my soul in Sheol, nor will You allow Your Holy One to see corruption." Acts 13:37 gives us the fulfillment of that prophecy: "But He whom God raised up saw no corruption." Even though Jesus was in the grave three days, His body did not decay or corrupt. Because He was sinless, they could not put Him to death. Instead, He laid down His life voluntarily that He could take it up again. He rose by His own power because death had no claim on Him.

First Corinthians 15 talks about the differences between Adam and Jesus. Starting in verse 47, we read,

> The first man was of the earth, made of dust; the second Man is the Lord from heaven. As was the man of dust, so also are those who are made of dust; and as is the heavenly Man, so also are those who are heavenly. And as we have borne the image of the man of dust, we shall also bear the image of the heavenly Man.

Verses 53–57 say,

> For this corruptible must put on incorruption, and this mortal must put on immortality. So when this corruptible has put on incorruption, and this mortal has put on immortality, then shall be brought to pass the saying that is written: *"Death is swallowed up in victory. O Death, where is your sting? O Hades, where is your victory?"* The sting of death is sin, and the strength of sin is the law. But thanks be to God, who gives us the victory through our Lord Jesus Christ.

Man cannot redeem man from sin and death. Romans 3:23 tells us clearly that we have all sinned. We cannot redeem ourselves since God decreed the sacrificial offering had to be sinless, or without blemish. Hebrews 9:22, 26b, and 28 say, "And according to the law almost all things are purified with blood, and without shedding of blood there is no remission... He has appeared to put away sin by the sacrifice of Himself...so Christ was offered once to bear the sins of many."

The only remedy for death is life. Where is life? In the Blood! Jesus's body was from the virgin Mary, but His blood was from His

Father in heaven. His sinless, supernatural blood is the only price of redemption that Father God can accept. Death can only be banished by life. We can "cheat" death for a while with blood transfusions, where one person's blood is put into another person. Interestingly, if sufficient blood is given to one person from one other person, it has been documented that the recipient will take on personality traits of the donor. The blood of Jesus changes us from sinners to saints. Scriptures never refer to a believer in Christ as a sinner—only as saints. Once accepting the salvation available through the blood of Jesus, the new believer embarks on a life of being changed to take on more and more of his Donor's personality. We are to become like Jesus.

After Christ made the atonement, He rose and ascended into heaven to present the blood in the Holy of Holies, according to Hebrews 9:24: "For Christ has not entered the holy places made with hands, which are copies of the true, but into heaven itself, now to appear in the presence of God for us." In the earthly Holy of Holies, there was no seat for the high priest. Yet Hebrews 10:12 and 14 tells us that Jesus is sitting: "But this Man, after He had offered one sacrifice for sins forever, sat down at the right hand of God...for by one offering He has perfected forever those who are being sanctified." Jesus did declare just before his death, "It is finished!" The work was finished once for all. The blood has been shed—the incorruptible, eternal, divine, sinless, overcoming, precious, unending blood of our Savior! The work of salvation and redemption has been finished, so our high priest can sit at the right hand of the Father. The blood of Jesus never loses its power.

The Line of the Blood

The Bible has a scarlet "thread" that runs through it from Genesis to Revelation. Genesis 3:21 holds the first mention about a sacrifice to atone for sin. God made tunics of skin and clothed them. The skin presumably came from animals, which were sacrificed to atone for the sin of Adam and Eve. From this first mention about atonement for sacrifice, we can learn three things:

1. Salvation (atonement) must be of the Lord. John 3:16 says, "For God so loved the world that He gave His only begotten Son, that whoever believes in Him should not perish but have everlasting life."

2. Salvation (atonement) must be by the death of an innocent substitute. First Peter 2:22–24 says,

> *Who committed no sin, nor was deceit found in His mouth,* who when He was reviled, did not revile in return; when He suffered, He did not threaten, but committed Himself to Him who judges righteously; who Himself bore our sins in His own body on the tree, that we, having died to sins, might live for righteousness—by whose stripes you were healed.

3. Salvation (atonement) must be by blood. First Peter 1:18–21 says,

> Knowing that you were not redeemed with corruptible things, like silver or gold, from your aimless conduct…but with the precious blood of Christ, as of a lamb without blemish and without spot. He indeed was foreordained before the foundation of the world, but was manifest in these last times for you who through Him believe in God, who raised Him from the dead and gave Him glory, so that your faith and hope are in God.

Abel's sacrifice met these three conditions, but Cain's did not. Cain brought a sacrifice of his own—just some of the fruit of the ground. Scripture doesn't even say that Cain brought the first of the fruit of the ground. Cain's offering was not the substitution of an innocent life for the sinful one. Abel's was, and he was justified before God by the shedding of its blood. It did not take long, only one generation, for sin to be rampant enough in the heart of man to commit murder.

The Lord must demand blood for the atonement of sin. The reason lies in the nature of God. God is perfect. God is holy. Our sin must be covered and satisfy the justice of God, so God gave Israel a holy, perfect, and just law at Mount Sinai. Disobedience to that law demanded the greatest penalty in payment. God, in His mercy, also gave Israel the Tabernacle to hold the Ark of the Covenant in the Holy of Holies. The Ark, an oblong box made of acacia wood and covered in gold, contained the Ten Commandments (representing all of the law) written on stone tablets. The top of the Ark had the Mercy Seat. Israel even broke the law while waiting for Moses to come down from Mount Sinai with the law from God. See Exodus 32:1. The broken law demanded the eternal damnation of Israel, but God had made provision for this. He knew we were all incapable of keeping the law. Once a year, on the Day of Atonement, the high priest took the blood of the animal sacrifice and sprinkled it on the Mercy Seat. God was appeased; atonement had been made for one year. God's justice was satisfied. His mercy could flow for another year onto His sinful people.

To look upon the broken law without blood is to face wrath. God said, "And when I see the blood, I will pass over you" (Exod. 12:13). God explained this principle of atonement to Adam and Eve, who were to pass it on to the next generation as an eternal principle. First Samuel 6:19 describes what happened when man removed the blood from God's righteous judgment—certain destruction: "Then He struck the men of Beth Shemesh, because they had looked into the ark of the LORD. He struck fifty thousand and seventy men of the people, and the people lamented because the LORD had struck the people with a great slaughter."

The necessity of innocent blood as atonement for sin is evident in how Moses dealt with the golden calf idol that Israel made. The people admitted that, "This Moses, the man who brought us up out of the land of Egypt, we do not know what has become of him" (Exod. 32:1). Tired of waiting, they decided to build gods to go before them. Aaron instructed them to bring all their gold (which they had plundered from the Egyptians at God's direction) to him. As Aaron told Moses in Exodus 32:24, "So they gave it to me, and I cast it into the fire, and this calf came out."

Moses knew that nothing but blood atonement could avert judgment for the children of Israel, who were unrestrained in idolatrous worship. Moses took the golden calf, melted it, ground it twice into fine powder, scattered the powder on the water of the brook, and made the Israelites drink it. Deuteronomy 9:21 as well as Exodus 32:20 give the details. Why did Moses go through all that trouble? The answer lies in chemistry.

In chemistry, there is one type of mixture called emulsion or suspension. Gold is nearly twenty times heavier than water and insoluble in water. As a fine powder, gold in water becomes a colloidal condition. There is no solution (where the added substance is dissolved and absorbed into the atomic structure of the water, increasing its weight but not its volume). The fine powdered gold particles are suspended between the water atoms. The gold suspended throughout the water gives the liquid a red color. Depending on the size of the gold powder particles, the color can range from deep red to rose red. The golden calf did not have to be huge to color enough water "bloodred" for two million or more people to drink it.

When Moses burned the golden calf, he removed the impurities from the gold. Thus, it was nontoxic to drink since the impurities had been burned out. Colloidal gold actually inhibits germs, just as colloidal silver does.

Even with all the effort and knowledge Moses applied to get the people to drink "the blood," he wasn't sure if it would actually work. Exodus 32:30 indicates this: "Now... Moses said to the people, 'You have committed a great sin. So now I will go up to the LORD; perhaps I can make atonement for your sin.'" Moses wasn't sure the blood-colored water would be sufficient. He was correct to say "perhaps" to the people. He interceded on their behalf, but God answered, "'Whoever has sinned against Me, I will blot him out of

My book... Nevertheless, in the day when I visit for punishment, I will visit punishment upon them for their sin.' So the LORD plagued the people because of what they did with the calf which Aaron made" (Exod. 32:33–35).

Exodus 32:25–28 suggests that three thousand men were totally unrestrained and apparently refused to drink the gold colloidal water. Moses made the atonement. God accepted it for those who drank it by faith. Christ died for all, but only those who choose to appropriate His provision are saved. It is a personal decision. As the old saying goes in America, "You can lead a horse to water, but you can't make him drink." That applies to salvation as evidenced in this story from Exodus. Drinking the "blood of Christ" has to be done by faith. Christ paid for our sins and wants to give life, peace, joy, hope, and victory to everyone who will humble himself or herself and drink it.

The Structure of the Blood

The blood in our body is fluid and moves throughout our bodies through the complicated system of arteries, veins, and capillaries to supply every cell with nourishment. It exchanges that nourishment for the cell's waste. Blood circulates throughout the entire body approximately every twenty-three seconds. Every cell is constantly supplied and cleansed by the blood, without contamination if the blood system remains closed. A wound or other "opening" of the blood system can bring in contamination. If the blood fails to reach certain cells or sections of the body, those cells or sections die. The blood is necessary for life. Man dies when his blood ceases to circulate.

As believers in Christ, we each are part of the body of Christ. Jesus is the head, according to Colossians 1:18: "And He is the head of the body, the church, who is the beginning, the firstborn from the dead, that in all things He may have the preeminence." All believers are related by the blood of Jesus. The life of each believer is dependent upon Jesus for life, nourishment, cleansing, and growth. Just as all mankind is related by Adam's sinful blood, part of the mystery and greatness of salvation is that we become brothers and sisters in Christ and of Christ. In Mark 3:33–35, Jesus asked, "'Who is My mother, or My brothers?' And He looked around in a circle at those who sat about Him, and said, 'Here are My mother and My brothers! For whoever does the will of God is My brother and My sister and mother.'" We are brothers and sisters of Jesus Christ, and we are brothers and sisters in the body of Jesus Christ. "There is neither Jew nor Greek, there is neither slave nor free, there is neither male nor female; for you are all one in Christ Jesus" according to Galatians 3:28. Also, Hebrews 2:11 says, "For both He who sanctifies and those who are being sanctified are all of one, for which reason He is not ashamed to call them brethren."

Just as the blood supplies our bodies with everything that it needs to live, grow, and thrive, it also carries off the "garbage" that needs to be eliminated from each cell in order to keep the body in good health. The same is true regarding our relationship with Jesus. He is our source for eternal life. His blood alone cleanses us from sin and washes the "garbage" out of our souls and bodies, minds, and wills as we yield to Him.

In times of infection, our white blood cells increase dramatically. They are carried by the blood to the site of infection. They surround the germs, engulfing and absorbing them. In essence, they are soldiers who die for the sake of the body's health. The blood of Jesus also helps us in times of attack by the enemy. Revelation 12:10–11 says,

> Now salvation, and strength and the kingdom of our God, and the power of His Christ have come, for the accuser of our brethren, who accused them before our God day and night, has been cast down. And they overcame him by the blood of the Lamb and by the word of their testimony, and they did not love their lives to the death.

The blood of Jesus is sufficient to overcome Satan when he accuses us in front of God. The blood of Jesus is also sufficient to overcome Satan when he accuses us in our own minds. The blood fights for us. We acknowledge our sin, and then we can claim the promise of 1 John 1:9: "If we confess our sins, He is faithful and just to forgive us our sins and to cleanse us from all unrighteousness." We can also claim 1 John 1:7: "But if we walk in the light as He is in the light, we have fellowship with one another, and the blood of Jesus Christ His Son cleanses us from all sin."

Antibodies in the blood help prevent disease. The body can build these up to prevent re-infection of a particular disease. It is this principle that makes immunizations work to prevent diseases. Similarly, the blood of Jesus helps us build up resistance to particular temptations that can be a downfall for an individual.

The blood is so powerful as the only acceptable atonement for sin that God ordered Noah to have extras of every clean animal and bird for an offering. Genesis 8:20–21 says,

> Then Noah built an altar to the LORD, and took of every clean animal and of every clean bird, and offered burnt offerings on the altar. And the LORD smelled a soothing aroma. Then the LORD said in His heart, "I will never again curse the ground for man's sake, although the imagination of man's heart is evil from his youth; not will I again destroy every living thing as I have done."

The Application of the Blood of Jesus

Demons are real. They get tired. They have memories. They have intelligence and work together. See Matthew 12:43–45, Luke 8:26–37, and Acts 19:13–16 for examples. Yet we have victory over demonic forces and over Satan who is the head of these demonic forces, by the blood of Jesus: "Behold, I give you the authority to trample on serpents and scorpions, and over all the power of the enemy, and nothing shall by any means hurt you" (Luke 10:19). First John 4:4 tells us, "You are of God, little children, and have overcome them, because He who is in you is greater than he who is in the world."

We have the weapon of the blood of Jesus, and can command Satan to take his hands off our family and all those we love. Job regularly applied the blood to all of his family (Job 1:5). Satan asked God, "Have you not made a hedge around him, around his household, and around all that he has on every side? You have blessed the work of his hands, and his possessions have increased in the land" (Job 1:10). You have to ask for God's protection. He supplies it, but it helps to ask for it. John 15:7 encourages us as Jesus says, "If you abide in Me, and My words abide in you, you will ask what you desire, and it shall be done for you."

It is our choice to abide. This is where free choice and free will of man comes in. We can choose to accept God or reject all He has done already for us. James 4:2 tells us that we have not because we do not ask God for it. Since all things are possible with God, there is no limit to what God can do for us through prayer—we have to ask.

God did all things for us at the cross. He gave us life (Eph. 2:5–6). He gave us grace and faith to believe in Him (Eph. 2:8–9). Jesus said, "Without Me you can do nothing" (John 15:5). We can't even come to God without God's help: "No one can come to Me unless the Father who sent Me draws him" (John 6:44). According to Philippians 2:13, "For it is God who works in you both to will and to do for His good pleasure." We are even too weak to hold onto God's hand. He holds ours. "For I, the LORD your God, will hold your right hand, saying to you, 'Fear not, I will help you'" (Isa. 41:13). "And I give them eternal life, and they shall never perish; neither shall anyone snatch them out of My hand. My Father, who has given them to Me, is greater than all; and no one is able to snatch them out of My Father's hand" (John 10:28–29). The only thing God wants from us is our surrender. He wants us to give Him our sins and be totally dependent upon Him. He is the only one capable of subduing our sins: "He will again have compassion on us, and will subdue our iniquities" (Micah 7:19).

Romans 8:2–4 sums this all up:

> For the law of the Spirit of life in Christ
> Jesus has made me free from the law of sin and

death. For what the law could not do in that it was weak through the flesh, God did by sending His own Son in the likeness of sinful flesh, on account of sin: He condemned sin in the flesh, that the righteous requirement of the law might be fulfilled in us who do not walk according to the flesh but according to the Spirit.

The blood of Jesus is the only thing that can redeem us from darkness and carry us into light. It alone atones for each and every sin. We have the privilege and choice to cover ourselves, our property and possessions, our loved ones, our thoughts, and our conversations with the blood of Jesus daily. His blood never runs out, and we can cover every single aspect of our lives with this powerful protection and cleansing agent each time we pray. What a joy! This is why we have faith and hope. We are cleansed, protected, healed, and redeemed by the blood. The enemy cannot cross the bloodline after we invoke it via prayer. It is by the blood that he is defeated.

12

HOLY SPIRIT

Holy Spirit is the third person of the triune God. He is not, of Himself, a weapon of warfare on our belt of truth but I feel that He is important enough to be included in this book. I do feel that the evidence of the baptism of Holy Spirit, the infilling of believers evidenced by the speaking in tongues, is a powerful weapon of offense and defense for believers to use. I have personally experienced the difference this baptism or infilling has made in my life. It was much greater than even describing it as the "scales being lifted off my eyes." My understanding of Scripture while reading it was incredibly different. I struggled and plodded before. I gave up trying to read it early on since I just couldn't understand it. After the baptism of Holy Spirit, it was so easy to read and understand. My discernment increased greatly too. The only way to describe it is like someone turned on all the lights. I was no longer stumbling around in the darkness, feeling my way. I could easily see instead.

Jesus spent a lot of His last words talking to His disciples about "another helper" for them since He knew His time had come. He was going to be crucified and then ascend to heaven. He was comforting His disciples, although they probably didn't understand at that time. He was also warning them of what was to come—persecution and hatred from "the world." He reiterated His love for each of them and the intimate relationship He wanted with them. He emphasized abiding in Himself, abiding in His love, bearing fruit, and giving the disciples His joy.

In John 14:16–18, He says,

> And I will pray the Father, and He will give
> you another Helper, that He may abide with you
> forever—the Spirit of truth, whom the world
> cannot receive, because it neither sees Him nor
> knows Him; but you know Him, for He dwells
> with you and will be in you. I will not leave you
> orphans; I will come to you.

In these verses, we have some great promises. Jesus promises here that Father God won't leave us. Jesus also says that He (Jesus) is coming to us. Then, Jesus said Spirit of truth, or Holy Spirit, will be beside us *and* in us.

These verses are proof of the Trinity—Father, Son, and Holy Spirit. All three are interconnected here, and all three are promised by Jesus to be with us and in us. All three are manifestations of the one God, like the three sides of a triangle are three different sides of one triangle. A different analogy would be like the three ways water appears: frozen (ice or snow), liquid (water that flows), or vapor (steam or humidity). All three are water, but in different forms.

Jesus was telling His disciples that a different form of Him would be coming to stay with them and in them. That would be different than just living with Jesus, beside Him. This would be better, but invisible: "You have heard Me say to you, 'I am going away and coming back to you.' If you loved Me, you would rejoice because I said, 'I am going to the Father,' for My Father is greater than I" (John 14:28). Jesus restated this a few moments later in John 16:7: "Nevertheless I tell you the truth. It is to your advantage that I go away; for if I do not go away, the Helper will not come to you; but if I depart, I will send Him to you."

God promises twelve different times in various forms in Scripture that He will never leave us nor forsake us. Jesus restates this promise in John 14:23: "If anyone loves Me, he will keep My word; and My Father will love him, and We will come to him and make Our home with him." The "we" and "our" Jesus is referring to here includes Father, Son, and Holy Spirit. He just finished saying Father was going to send another comforter or helper to the believers. If we love Jesus, we will keep His word. Father God will love us. Father God and Jesus will come to the believer, send Holy Spirit to dwell with us and in us, and make their home with the believer. This is what I am talking about with the infilling or baptism of Holy Spirit.

Why do we describe it as a baptism? Luke 3:16 calls it that "John answered, saying to all, 'I indeed baptize you with water; but One mightier than I is coming, whose sandal strap I am not worthy to loose. He will baptize you with the Holy Spirit and fire.'" Matthew 3:11 also says, "I indeed baptize you with water unto repentance, but He who is coming after me is mightier than I, whose sandals I am not worthy to carry. He will baptize you with the Holy Spirit and fire."

Water baptism is a baptism of repentance and also an important weapon of defense against enemy attacks. Our eldest son had received the baptism of Holy Spirit at a young age, with the evidence of speaking in tongues, but had not been baptized in water. As one friend put it, it was like putting a jet engine on a tricycle. The enemy began to harass him to the point that he actually saw Satan himself trying to attack him. We had been on a business trip when we received the call where he described what happened to him in that situation. My husband cancelled the rest of the business meetings and we flew home right away. The weird spiritual attacks stopped once he was also baptized with water.

These scriptures make it clear, though, that there is a separate baptism of Holy Spirit possible for each believer and expected to be received. John says that Jesus "will baptize you with the Holy Spirit and fire." That's a positive statement: *will*, not "maybe" or "might" or even "probably." However, just as we have to choose to be baptized with water, we need to choose these baptisms too. I believe that fire baptism is yet to come and is not the same as baptism of Holy Spirit.

Jesus emphasized the importance of being baptized in Holy Spirit in Acts 1:4–5: "And being assembled together with them, He commanded them not to depart from Jerusalem, but to wait for the Promise of the Father, 'which,' He said, 'you have heard from Me; for John truly baptized with water, but you shall be baptized with the Holy Spirit not many days from now.'"

Man reflects God in that we are made up of three parts too: body, soul, and spirit. Our body is our flesh. We can be tall, short, round, thin, dark, light, with different color hair and eyes. These are all aspects of our bodies. Our soul is our total personality. It is made up of our mind, will, and emotions. It is invisible and cannot be seen by any natural means. Our spirit is our innermost being, as the Bible calls it. We tend to think of our spirit as being located in our heart or in our belly. The spirit of a person is also invisible and cannot be seen by any natural means. We are somewhat in charge of our bodies, in that our brain tells our arm or foot to move. God is still ultimately in charge of our bodies, in that He is the One who keeps the automatic parts of our bodies working, such as our brains, our heart beating, our nervous system, our eye's ability to focus automatically. We have a choice to make regarding who is in charge of the invisible us. If our soul is in charge, that means we are in charge. Acting out of soulish desires will always get us in trouble spiritually because we are listening to our own selfish desires. God is not in charge if our soul is. To totally allow God to have charge of us, we need to yield our soul to Him. We need to allow God, or Holy Spirit into our soul to rule us.

This is where the baptism of Holy Spirit comes in. The baptism of Holy Spirit can also be termed the release of Holy Spirit into our souls. Ephesians 5:18 urges us to "be filled with the Spirit." First Thessalonians 5:23 says, "Now may the God of peace Himself sanctify you completely; and may your whole spirit, soul, and body be preserved blameless at the coming of our Lord Jesus Christ." After salvation, what needs to be filled? Our souls. At salvation, Holy Spirit fills that empty void spot often called the "God shaped hole" in our heart or our spirit. Our soul can then choose to be large and in charge, or we can allow Holy Spirit to be released into our souls, filling it with His desires, not ours.

The baptism of Holy Spirit is not for cleansing from sin, but for the purpose of empowering us for service to God—empowering us to live right. Jesus gave the purpose for this baptism when talking with the disciples in Acts 1:8: "But you shall receive power when the Holy Spirit has come upon you; and you shall be witnesses to Me in Jerusalem, and in all Judea and Samaria, and to the end of the earth."

Acts 2:1–4 records when the disciples received this gift:

> When the Day of Pentecost had fully come, they were all with one accord in one place. And suddenly there came a sound from heaven, as of a rushing mighty wind, and it filled the whole house where they were sitting. Then there appeared to them divided tongues, as of fire, and one sat upon each of them. And they were all filled with the Holy Spirit and began to speak with other tongues, as the Spirit gave them utterance.

Others heard them speaking words of God in their own languages. That is called speaking in tongues. The term "speaking in tongues" actually has two meanings. The more common meaning refers to a personal spiritual prayer language. The other meaning of speaking in tongues refers to times like in Acts 2 where Holy Spirit translates between the speaker's mouth and the hearer's ear so the hearer can understand the gospel message.

The woman who discipled me immediately after my baptism of Holy Spirit experience told me about her husband. He spoke in tongues with only a single phrase that sounded like "icky nicky." He asked for more prayer language, but that was all he got for some time. He decided to be obedient and continued saying that phrase over and over whenever he prayed in tongues. His unspoken thoughts were more along the lines of "Really, God? That's it?" He could only say that one phrase until he and his wife were in a foreign country on an evangelism crusade. The group began to pray in tongues on stage and with microphones, and so he did too since he was part of that group. He faithfully and obediently just kept repeating "icky nicky" over and over. He discovered that one man came forward for salvation based on hearing "icky nicky." That man lived far away in a remote area. He had heard about the crusade and walked for days to get there. In his local language, "icky nicky" meant Jesus loves you. He heard it and responded. After that event, the husband of my mentor was given a much more extensive spiritual prayer language.

There are Old Testament prophecies concerning speaking in tongues. Isaiah 28:11–12 is an example: "For with stammering lips and another tongue He will speak to this people, to whom He said, 'This is the rest with which you may cause the weary to rest,' and 'This is the refreshing'; yet they would not hear." My personal spiritual prayer language sounds, in part, like stammering.

I was once at a meeting, though, where Holy Spirit just descended and took over. There was an intense atmosphere of worship, awe, and intercession. Words were coming forth from the attendees from every part of the auditorium, one after another. Interpretations of those words given in tongues were also coming from all over the room. They all flowed together, though, so I know it was Holy Spirit directed. The speakers stopped teaching and talking. One word that came forth in tongues was actually in Spanish. I had just finished taking three years of Spanish and recognized it. There was an interpretation of that word given in English by someone else.

The Scripture of Isaiah 28:12 also indicates the choice believers have to accept the gift, the refreshing, and rest that God offers in this baptism. Some will choose not to hear or receive it. I have read stories of people who went to heaven and then came back to Earth. They describe a river that people can submerge in for cleansing, healing, and restoration. It is so full of life that we can actually breathe that water. We don't have to hold our breath like when we swim here on Earth. We can breathe just like normal while being totally under the water in heaven. Jesus said rivers of living water would flow out of the heart of those who believe in Him (see John 7:37–38). I believe that speaking in tongues is a tiny portion of that river that flows from Jesus and through our hearts. Some believers have developed the discipline of speaking in tongues for fifteen minutes to an hour or more every day. I try and follow this discipline. I find that I hear God better when I do this, and I discern better. I have more energy and feel a refreshing when I do this. Simply put, I am more sensitive to the Spirit when I consistently practice praying in tongues.

Speaking in tongues is a powerful weapon of warfare and available for us to use. Because the disciples anticipated and received the gift of the baptism of Holy Spirit, three thousand believers were added to their group that first day. First Corinthians 14:21 refers to this prophecy in Isaiah, too: "In the law it is written: '*With men of other tongues and other lips I will speak to this people; and yet, for all that, they will not hear Me.*'" That passage goes on to talk about the spiritual prayer language most commonly referred to as speaking in tongues in the church.

Joel also prophesied about this baptism, which Peter referred to as recorded in Acts 2:16–19 and 21:

> But this is what was spoken by the prophet Joel: "*And it shall come to pass in the last days, says God, that I will pour out of My Spirit on all flesh; your sons and your daughters shall prophesy, your young men shall see visions, your old men shall dream dreams. And on My menservants and on My maidservants I will pour out My Spirit in those days; and they shall prophesy. I will show wonders in heaven above and signs in the earth beneath... and it shall come to pass that whoever calls on the name of the LORD shall be saved.*"

There are other references in Acts and 1 Corinthians to the baptism of Holy Spirit with the evidence of speaking in tongues:

> Then Peter said to them, "Repent, and let every one of you be baptized in the name of Jesus Christ for the remission of sins; and you shall receive the gift of the Holy Spirit. For the promise is to you and to your children, and to all who are afar off, as many as the Lord our God will call." (Acts 2:38–39)

> Now when the apostles who were at Jerusalem heard that Samaria had received the word of God, they sent Peter and John to them, who, when they had come down, prayed for

them that they might receive the Holy Spirit. For as yet He had fallen upon none of them. They had only been baptized in the name of the Lord Jesus. Then they laid hands on them, and they received the Holy Spirit. [This verse again proves that there is a difference between baptism for repentance and belief in Jesus versus the baptism of Holy Spirit.] (Acts 8:14–17)

And Ananias went his way and entered the house; and laying his hands on him he said, "Brother Saul, the Lord Jesus, who appeared to you on the road as you came, has sent me that you may receive your sight and be filled with the Holy Spirit." (Acts 9:17)

First Corinthians 14:18 records that Paul did receive the baptism of Holy Spirit with the evidence of speaking in tongues: "I thank my God I speak with tongues more than you all."

Acts 10:12–48 records where the baptism of Holy Spirit was poured out on Gentiles for the first time. Verses 44–48 say,

While Peter was still speaking these words, the Holy Spirit fell upon all those who heard the word. And those of the circumcision who believed were astonished, as many as came with Peter, because the gift of the Holy Spirit had been poured out on the Gentiles also. For they heard them speak with tongues and magnify God. Then Peter answered, "Can anyone forbid water, that these should not be baptized who have received the Holy Spirit just as we have?" And he commanded them to be baptized in the name of the Lord.

Paul also baptized people in the Holy Spirit, as shown in Acts 19:5–6: "When they heard this, they were baptized in the name of the

Lord Jesus. And when Paul had laid hands on them, the Holy Spirit came upon them, and they spoke with tongues and prophesied."

The reason for accepting this gift from Jesus is to enable us to draw closer to God and to have personal, interactive relationship with Father, Son, and Holy Spirit. Through this gift, each believer can have God's supernatural power flowing through you so you can fully accomplish God's will in your life. For example, I was recently in a foreign country and purchased something in a store. As the clerk handed me my purchase, God (Holy Spirit) showed me that she had a problem with her shoulder. I knew she had limited ability to move her arm as a result. I knew all this in a flash, but had not seen evidence of it during her helping me in the store. I asked her about it and pointed to the shoulder with the problem. Language was a barrier, but her eyes got big, and she said yes, indicating she did have a problem. She asked if I was a doctor. I said no and tried to tell her that God revealed it to me. I was wearing my cross necklace and finally just lifted up the cross and said, "God showed me." I prayed for healing of her shoulder.

While I was praying, I actually felt God touching her. I love that feeling! But I only get to experience it some of the times when I pray with someone. Most times, I feel nothing, although the people receiving prayer often feel touched. At the end of the prayer, I asked her how her shoulder was and moved my arm to indicate how she should move hers. She did and said her shoulder was now fine. Mostly, she just stared at me with eyes huge with amazement (I hope!). In the end, again due to language barriers, I lifted up my cross and pointed upward to heaven and said, "Jesus healed you." The wonderful encounter was only possible because I could hear the small nudging of Holy Spirit telling me things I could not know on my own. Not even doctors can heal; they can only treat symptoms and get the body to a state where it heals naturally. Only Jesus truly heals. That supernatural power is through Holy Spirit.

The baptism of Holy Spirit helps us become Christ-like. He helps us understand Scripture and the things of God. He helps us live properly and victoriously. He helps us overcome. Holy Spirit gives us refreshing and strength, peace and rest for our spirit and soul. We don't have to walk around troubled, worried, or uneasy.

Jesus explains some of these benefits to his disciples in that last long conversation with them just before His arrest:

> But the Helper, the Holy Spirit, whom the Father will send in My name, He will teach you all things, and bring to your remembrance all things that I said to you. (John 14:26)

> But when the Helper comes, whom I shall send to you from the Father, the Spirit of truth who proceeds from the Father, He will testify of Me. And you also will bear witness, because you have been with Me from the beginning. (John 15:26–27)

In John 16:13–14, Jesus also talks about the reason He wants us to have this gift: "However, when He, the Spirit of truth, has come, He will guide you into all truth; for He will not speak on His own authority, but whatever He hears He will speak; and He will tell you things to come."

The baptism of Holy Spirit also gives us the benefit of increasing our ability to speak to God: "For he who speaks in a tongue does not speak to men but to God, for no one understands him; however, in the spirit he speaks mysteries." (1 Cor 14:2)

Furthermore, we edify ourselves, or improve our mind and character, when we speak in tongues. We charge ourselves up spiritually: "He who speaks in a tongue edifies himself." (1 Cor.14:4)

I had been praying for a while about my desire to hear God better. While in chaplain training, another student shared with me at lunch about speaking in tongues daily. I knew this was my answer from God. Praying in tongues daily has increased my sensitivity to Holy Spirit and enabled me to "hear" much better. I sometimes do it with my morning coffee and personal time with God. I pray in tongues when I am alone driving in my car. My friend prayed in tongues while getting ready for work each morning. There are ways to fit it into your daily life. The student who shared with me said that he actually wore a stopwatch around his neck. When he got on a bus, he started the stopwatch and prayed in tongues quietly until he had to stop. Then he stopped the stopwatch. As he found little increments of time during the day, he kept track of it on the stopwatch. He was praying in tongues more than half an hour each day. Since God is with us wherever we go, we don't have to be sitting still in holy quiet to be talking to Him in our prayer language. It is for our benefit that we do pray in tongues. Jude 20–21 says so: "But you, beloved, building yourselves up on your most holy faith, praying in the Holy Spirit, keep yourselves in the love of God, looking for the mercy of our Lord Jesus Christ unto eternal life."

If we don't even know what to pray—and there have been many times I've been in this situation—we are to pray in tongues. Romans 8:26–27 says,

> Likewise the Spirit also helps in our weaknesses. For we do not know what we should pray for as we ought, but the Spirit Himself makes intercession for us with groanings which cannot be uttered. Now He who searches the hearts knows what the mind of the Spirit is, because He makes intercession for the saints according to the will of God.

Our spiritual prayer language is the language of Holy Spirit given to us. I urge you to carefully reread that Scripture and ponder it. That should build up your faith, hope, and joy—knowing that God Himself, as Holy Spirit, continually intercedes for you!

Just as Jesus comforted, taught, and encouraged the disciples, Holy Spirit now does that for us. After receiving the free gift of the baptism of Holy Spirit, we enjoy relationship with the form of God that helps us live the way that Jesus was talking about. Holy Spirit is our advocate, encourager, comforter, teacher, counselor, and helper. Holy Spirit gives us good advice, wise instruction, and moral support. Holy Spirit helps us remember, understand, and live by Jesus's commands. Holy Spirit is the power from God to live in holiness.

Jesus promised that He would send this Helper. Second Peter 1:3–4 talks about this powerful promise that enables us to live in holiness:

> As His divine power has given to us all things that pertain to life and godliness, through the knowledge of Him who called us by glory and virtue, by which have been given to us exceedingly great and precious promises, that through these you may be partakers of the divine nature, having escaped the corruption that is in the world through lust.

Holy Spirit gives us the power to live in holiness. Holy Spirit gives us everything we need for life and godliness, so we can participate in the divine nature. This all comes through our knowledge of Jesus.

Jesus is the only way to God the Father because Jesus alone is the only one in all of history to deal with mankind's sin problem. Holy Spirit helps us understand the Bible. The world at large cannot receive Holy Spirit; He lives with us and in us. He teaches us; He reminds us of Jesus's words. He convicts us of sin, shows us God's way, and tells us what He hears the Father say. He guides us into truth and gives us insight into future events and into things we could not possibly know naturally. He brings glory to Christ. He helps us pray when we don't know how to pray.

What do you think all these benefits do to the enemy's plans for our lives? That's why the baptism of Holy Spirit with the evidence of speaking in tongues is such a powerful weapon. Simply put, it says "No!" to the enemy. Galatians 5:16 instructs us, "I say then: Walk in the Spirit, and you shall not fulfill the lust of the flesh." It goes on to talk about the lusts of the flesh that war against the Spirit. It also lists the fruit of the Spirit. This is an important passage summarizing our soulish flesh problem and the wonderful solution to it. I recommend you read Galatians 5:16–26 fully. Holy Spirit enables us to crucify our flesh and produce the fruit of holiness. God calls us to holy living, and He also provides the power for us to fulfill the call He gives us. He's amazing!

This was promised in Jeremiah 31:33: "But this is the covenant that I will make with the house of Israel after those days, says the LORD: I will put My law in their minds, and write it on their hearts; and I will be their God, and they shall be My people."

How does this happen? Ezekiel 36:26–27 says, "I will give you a new heart and put a new spirit within you; I will take the heart of stone out of your flesh and give you a heart of flesh. I will put My Spirit within you and cause you to walk in My statutes, and you will keep My judgments and do them."

Romans 5:1, 2, and 5 says,

> Therefore, having been justified by faith, we have peace with God through our Lord Jesus Christ, through whom also we have access by faith into this grace in which we stand, and rejoice in hope of the glory of God… Now hope does not disappoint, because the love of God has been poured out in our hearts by the Holy Spirit who was given to us.

The gift of Holy Spirit, sent by Jesus to us, is to help us know the love God has for us. Holy Spirit is the method by which Father God pours His love into our hearts. We obey His rules, His statutes, and His laws because of love.

I remember reading 2 Corinthians 1:21–22 while flying on a plane somewhere: "Now He who establishes us with you in Christ and has anointed us is God, who also has sealed us and given us the Spirit in our hearts as a guarantee." Because of things that happened to me in my childhood, I had a hard time just accepting the love that Father extends to me always. I couldn't understand it and had difficulty receiving it. I had a litany of other words and experiences that contradicted what Scripture was saying regarding my worth in God's eyes. The deposit of Holy Spirit into my heart proved to me time after time that Father did indeed guarantee His love for me. I needed the baptism of Holy Spirit! Every time I examine that wonderful guarantee or deposit, in my heart I think I add to that deposit every time I pray in tongues. I continually build up the savings in my heart and can see the compound growth adding up within me.

Holy Spirit gives us faith too. Galatians 3:2 and 5 says, "Did you receive the Spirit by the works of the law, or by the hearing of faith?... Therefore He who supplies the Spirit to you and works miracles among you, does He do it by the works of the law, or by the hearing of faith?" Holy Spirit helps our faith, increasing it as we grow with Jesus.

Holy Spirit gives us gifts to help the overall body, not just ourselves. Think what that does to the enemy's plans for the world! Hebrews 2:4 talks of signs, wonders, miracles, and gifts of the Spirit being distributed according to Father's will. First Corinthians 12:4–11 lists the primary gifts of the Spirit. Each of these gifts is a weapon against the enemy. They include the following:

1. Word of wisdom: Enabling the believer to give advice to someone who needs just that piece of advice.
2. Word of knowledge: Enabling the believer to know something that only God would know, not the believer operating in that gift, to prove He is God to the person receiving the Word of Knowledge. It is for the receiver's benefit, to help them, not for gossip.
3. Gift of faith: Giving a believer supernatural faith to accomplish something really big.
4. Gifts of healings: Power from God flowing through the believer to provide healing for the recipient, either a believer or an unbeliever (at that moment).
5. Gift of working of miracles: This is the something really big that is often accomplished: some supernatural event that cannot be explained by natural methods.
6. Gift of prophecy: Giving a believer insight into the future which he speaks out either to an individual, a group, or the

entire body. Prophecies can be for individuals, or they can tell the church body what is coming. They can be verbal, or it can also be a prophetic act of some kind.

7. Gift of discerning of spirits: Enabling the believer to know when angels or demonic forces are around or involved in a situation. Think of this as laser guided warfare.

8. Gift of speaking in tongues: This is the tongues where a hearer is able to hear in his own language what the speaker is saying, whether or not the speaker is talking in that language.

9. Gift of interpretation of tongues: Enabling a believer to speak in the local language the word that either that believer or another has uttered in a spiritual language in a group setting.

10. There are also gifts of Holy Spirit for the overall church, including teaching, preaching, administration, and others. You can see how all this can defeat the enemy and glorify God. The baptism of Holy Spirit enables the believer to walk in holiness, love, wisdom, faith, anointing to accomplish God's will—the list just goes on.

I have included in an appendix a prayer of repentance, salvation, and baptism of Holy Spirit with the evidence of speaking in tongues for those who need a sample to go by. It is only a guide. You do not have to pray it exactly that way to receive the baptism of Holy Spirit. Prayer is just talking to God, so relax and talk to Him. He wants to be your friend. He wants to pour His love into you via Holy Spirit.

It is so fun to work for God and experience and watch what He does when we obey that very quiet voice of Holy Spirit. It is such a joy to truly know how much Father loves us. Without Holy Spirit, we cannot have faith. With Holy Spirit, we have faith, hope, and joy.

13

OTHER WEAPONS ON OUR BELT OF TRUTH

You don't pull out a mousetrap to catch in elephant. You don't shoot a cannon to kill a mosquito either. It's really not a good idea to use a flamethrower to get the small spider on the wall of your house. These are all examples of ineffective or inappropriate tools (weapons) to get a job done. God has given us many more weapons of warfare that we can use to defeat the enemy, protect our loved ones and others, enlarge His kingdom on Earth as it is in heaven, and be the effective, efficient, obedient, and victorious soldier God desires each of us to be.

There are many incredible books already written about some of the weapons of warfare on our belt. Whole shelves, maybe even rooms full of books have been written on the blood of Jesus, for example. Listed in this chapter are some of the other weapons I have used, but I will only briefly touch on them. A few are weapons I feel you should know about, but I have seldom used them. They are "special" weapons. Most of these are weapons that I feel others have done such thorough jobs of covering as a single topic of a book, so I briefly mention them here and urge you to read and study more with other authors.

Praise

Praise means to confess, to proclaim, to acknowledge or declare God's character and God's works. The emphasis of praise lies in the recognition and the declaration of a fact. For believers, praise is the recognition of who God is and the declaration of what great things He has done: His attributes, His actions, His character, and His works.

For example, Exodus 15:1–21 records the song the Israelites spontaneously burst out singing when they successfully crossed the Red Sea on dry land, then turned to see their enemy swallowed up by that same sea. Imagine the awe the children of Israel had to have felt—scurrying across on seabed between two enormous walls of water with Pharaoh and his army right behind them. Were whales looking at them as they walked through? Maybe a shark or octopus?

I've been to the Red Sea and visited the aquarium at Eilat. Instead of building a tank for the various species of fish, that aquarium was designed as a tank to hold humans in the water. The various fish and sea creatures swim around free and natural while you can observe them through the glass walls of an underground room submerged into the Red Sea. It was spectacular to visit. I saw beautiful corals and a "plant" that looked like a single huge white rose blooming. Scripture doesn't record that God pushed the coral out of the way, only the water. The seabed may have been dry for the Israelites to walk across, but it probably wasn't a paved, smooth road. Scrambling around corals would have been difficult terrain to walk across with an enemy breathing down their neck. The Israelites had to have experienced fear, awe, difficulty, and then immeasurable relief as their enemy was drowned as they gave pursuit. No wonder they burst into song!

Hebrew is a language with few words, but multiple meanings to each word, as compared to the English language. Old Hebrew (biblical) has approximately 1,500 different roots and approximately 8,000 words according to one source. Modern Hebrew has between 60,000 and 150,000 words. In comparison, English has over 1 million words.

In the Hebrew language of few words, there are at least fourteen that translate as "praise." This subject is important since so many different words are used to specify specific differences in praise. Halal, one of those fourteen words, means to praise, to shout or cry aloud, or to shout for joy. We get hallelujah from this Hebrew word, which could be said as "halal yah" or "praise Yehovah." It is a command by the way. Psalm 117:1 commands, "Praise the LORD, all you Gentiles! Laud Him, all you peoples!"

Do not confuse the method of praise, or the expression of praise, for the praise itself. While I may not like some of the songs sung in corporate settings as praise to God, I cannot argue with the praise itself. Praise is proclaiming, acknowledging, or declaring God's character and God's works. That is what I should focus on, instead of my dislike of a particular beat, musical style, action, volume, tempo, or key.

There is power when we worship or praise God. When we bow before the one true God, He becomes the lifter of our heads and lifts us up into a proper position where He wants us. He does this because we are no longer slaves to the enemy. We are no longer slaves to our sin. He lifts our head because we are His good and faithful servants, acceptable to Him because of Jesus. When we praise God, it naturally combats our inclination toward idolatry. It puts God at the center of your world. It trains you to look at the Son rather than at yourself. Praise with thanksgiving is actually an act of repentance—it is a continual turning from self to God.

The enemy hates it when we praise God. Satan has been trying to get our praise and worship ever since he fell from heaven. The battle really is over our worship. We praise God with words, with thanksgiving, with song, and with musical instruments.

We can praise him with dance. Miriam did in Exodus 15:20. We can praise Him with uplifted hands. Psalm 63:3–4 says, "Because Your lovingkindness is better than life, my lips shall praise You. Thus I will bless You while I live; I will lift up my hands in Your name." Psalm 134:2 commands "Lift up your hands in the sanctuary, and bless the LORD." Psalm 141:2 says, "Let my prayer be set before You as incense, the lifting up of my hands as the evening sacrifice."

We can praise Him with bended knee, or standing, or sitting, or flat on our face. We can praise Him with shouting and clapping: "Oh, clap your hands, all you peoples! Shout to God with the voice of triumph! For the LORD Most High is awesome; He is a great king over all the earth. He will subdue the peoples under us, and the nations under our feet" (Ps. 47:1–3). Clapping can also be an act of disdain for the enemy, as in Lamentations 2:15: "All who pass by clap their hands at you; they hiss and shake their heads." In this reference, the enemy is exhibiting disdain for God's people. However, the enemy can only imitate, not create. Thus, we know we also can clap our hands in disdain at the enemy, as well as in praise to God.

There are at least twelve different words in Scripture for "shout." Remember, a lion roars, so the Lion of Judah also roars. The Lord Himself speaks with a shout, as in Numbers 23:21: "He has not observed iniquity in Jacob, nor has He seen wickedness in Israel. The LORD his God is with him, and the shout of a king is among them." Psalm 47:5 also says that God shouts, "God has gone up with a shout, the LORD with the sound of a trumpet." Jeremiah 25:30 also talks about God roaring and shouting: "The LORD will roar from on high, and utter His voice from His holy habitation; He will roar mightily." Psalm 78:65–66 says, "Then the Lord awoke as from sleep, like a mighty man who shouts because of wine. And He beat back His enemies; He put them to a perpetual reproach."

Sometimes, we just have to roar. I was speaking at a Liberian congregation, and God told me to have the people roar at their problems. So I instructed them to shout and roar like the Lion of Judah at their problems. It was powerful, and we roared long enough to have sore throats as a result. Another speaker came up to me to ask if I knew the power of what I had done. One look at my face told that speaker I did not. They were right. I had no idea how powerful that time of roaring at our problems would be for each person there that night. I just did what God told me to do. He said to do it, so I just trusted and assumed it would be exactly what each person needed. Even Jesus shouted. See Matthew 27:50, Mark 15:34, Luke 23:46 for examples.

What is important is to remember to praise Him at all times. While God does want us to remember what He did in the past, such as at the exodus from Egypt, the far past works are not the only things He wants us to praise Him for. When we praise Him about throwing the horse and rider into the sea, it reminds us that God can do the same thing for our problem since He is no respecter of persons. What He did for the Israelites, He desires to do for us also.

Here's an example of what I mean. I was cleaning out old files in my desk and ran across a folder of my daughter's certificates and awards from grade school. She was a great student and won many academic recognitions, including some national awards from a presidential program. They were important to her, valuable at the time, so we saved them. Now, twenty some years later, those rewards don't have the same value or meaning. If I continued to praise her for those sixth-grade awards while ignoring the academic scholarships she received to get her doctorate degree, I would be silly.

The same principle applies to our praise of God. Keep your eyes on Him and watch for things to praise Him for. He delights to give us gifts and love presents, as well as rescue us in a mighty display of His power. Praise Him for the little blessings in your life. Praise Him for the gifts He gives you, like a beautiful sunrise or sunset, a shooting star, or some other sight in nature. Praise Him for anything and everything. I decided one morning on the way to church to just start listing out loud all the things I was thankful for to God. My husband and I took turns listing things. We did not repeat each other's lists either. We weren't finished at the end of our thirty-minute drive to get to church. If we have a heart of thanksgiving and live in praise, incredible things will happen to us. It is a powerful weapon of warfare.

Laughter

Along with praise and thanksgiving, laughter is actually a weapon of warfare. Second Kings 19:21 says, "This is the word which the LORD has spoken concerning him: 'The virgin, the daughter of Zion, has despised you, laughed you to scorn; the daughter of Jerusalem has shaken her head behind your back!'" King Hezekiah had received a letter from Sennacherib. The king of Assyria was waging war to increase his kingdom, and Israel was in his sights. Hezekiah took the letter into the temple to pray to God for help. Isaiah spoke God's answer to Hezekiah and said the daughters of Jerusalem would laugh Sennacherib to scorn. We can just laugh at the enemy sometimes. It is very frustrating to try and intimidate someone who just laughs at you and refuses to become ruffled or afraid. The enemy laughs at us (Job 41:29 says the leviathan laughs at his enemy's attempts to kill him) so we can use the same weapon against him. If we get the concept of just how big, how powerful, how loving our God is, we can laugh at a lot of the enemy's attempts to take us out of the fight. We've got a very big Daddy standing right behind us.

Ecclesiastes 3:4 says there is a time to laugh. This would include warfare, not just celebration or fun times. Psalm 52:6–7 says, "The righteous also shall see and fear, and shall laugh at him, saying, 'Here is the man who did not make God his strength, but trusted in the abundance of his riches, and strengthened himself in his wickedness.'" Laughter can be a laugh of happiness or a laugh of scorn. Job records in chapter 8:19–21, "Behold, this is the joy of His way… Behold, God will not cast away the blameless, nor will He uphold the evildoers. He will yet fill your mouth with laughing, and your lips with rejoicing." What is the result of this laughter? Verse 22 says, "Those who hate you will be clothed with shame, and the dwelling place of the wicked will come to nothing."

Psalm 126:2 shows the power of laughter again. "Then our mouth was filled with laughter, and our tongue with singing. Then they said among the nations, 'The LORD has done great things for them.'" When we laugh at the enemy, those observing have to acknowledge that the LORD has done great things for us. When should we rejoice?

1. *In famine.* Though the fig tree may not blossom, nor fruit be on the vines; though the labor of the olive may fail, and the fields yield no food; though the flock may be cut off from the fold, and there be no herd in the stalls—yet I will

rejoice in the LORD, I will joy in the God of my salvation. The LORD God is my strength; He will make my feet like deer's feet, and He will make me walk on my high hills. (Hab. 3:17–19)

2. *In persecution.* "Blessed are you when men hate you, and when they exclude you, and revile you, and cast out your name as evil, for the Son of Man's sake. Rejoice in that day and leap for joy! For indeed your reward is great in heaven" (Luke 6:22–23).

3. *In suffering.* "I now rejoice in my sufferings for you, and fill up in my flesh what is lacking in the afflictions of Christ, for the sake of His body, which is the church" (Col. 1:24).

4. *In loss of possessions.* "For you...joyfully accepted the plundering of your goods, knowing that you have a better and an enduring possession for yourselves in heaven. Therefore do not cast away your confidence, which has great reward" (Heb. 10:34–35).

5. *In fiery trials.* Beloved, do not think it strange concerning the fiery trial which is to try you, as though some strange thing happened to you; but rejoice to the extent that you partake of Christ's sufferings, that when His glory is revealed, you may also be glad with exceeding joy. (1 Pet. 4:12–14)

Laughter, in joy, can also be a weapon of defense against disease and decay, which are results of original sin and not God's original design for our bodies. Abraham is our example of this. Abraham laughed in Genesis 17:15–17. Verse 17 records, "Then Abraham fell on his face and laughed, and said in his heart, 'Shall a child be born to a man who is one hundred years old? And shall Sarah, who is ninety years old, bear a child?'" Sarah not only bore a son, she nursed him. She was 127 years old when she died, so she lived approximately thirty-seven years after Isaac's birth. Abraham was 137 when Sarah died. He married Keturah and had six more sons. Abraham died at the age of 175. His son Isaac (laughter) was sixty years old when Rebekah bore Esau and Jacob (Gen. 25:26). This means Abraham was 160 years old when the twins were born. The twins were fifteen when Abraham died. Proverbs 17:22 says, "A merry heart does good, like medicine, but a broken spirit dries the bones."

Why does the Bible record that Sarah laughed when she over-heard God's conversation with Abraham about her soon-to-be-con-ceived baby? The Hebrew for the word *dries* in Proverbs 17:22 means "to dry up, confuse, confound, shame, wither away." The word in that verse for "bones" means "the body, the strength, the bones," according to *Strong's Concordance*. Hebrews 11:11 says, "Sarah herself also received strength to conceive seed, and she bore a child when she was past the age, because she judged Him faithful who had prom-ised." Sarah laughed (Gen. 18:12). I personally think that was part of God strengthening her body with her merry heart to start the process of reversing time so she could conceive. I can just imagine Abraham and Sarah talking in the evenings about God's promise and laughing for the joy of that promise to them. It says that Sarah *her-self* also received strength to conceive. Sarah and Abraham lived very long lives and experienced joy and laughter to the point they named their son Isaac, which means laughter. Joy and laughter are powerful weapons for us, both offensively and defensively.

These weapons—praise, singing, musical instruments, danc-ing, uplifted hands, laughing, shouting, and/or clapping all serve to encourage us, which also is a weapon of warfare. When we are encouraged, when we keep or turn our focus on the LORD instead of our problem, the enemy and the problem are automatically dimin-ished and become smaller when compared to the greatness of God. That encouragement helps us to keep fighting.

Treading, Walking, or Marching

Psalm 108:13 talks about treading as a warfare tactic: "Through God we will do valiantly, for it is He who shall tread down our ene-mies." Jesus talked to his disciples about treading (trampling) on the enemy too. Luke 10:19 records Jesus saying, "Behold, I give you the authority to trample on serpents and scorpions, and over all the power of the enemy, and nothing shall by any means hurt you."

Treading is very much like marching, only more aggressive. You can combine treading, or aggressive marching, around a property while praising, driving stakes into the ground at the corners of the property or some other method of marking the property lines, and praying to apply the precious blood of Jesus along the border of the property. You can even make the barrier of the blood high, like a wall. Similarly, a spiritual hedge of thorns can be prayed as a wall of protection around whomever or whatever you are praying protection over. Just as God made walls out of the water so the children of Israel could cross the Red Sea on dry land, you can pray walls of protection that reach up to heaven. In the case of a wayward child, the spiritual hedge of thorns and blood of Jesus walls prevent or discourage the enemy from getting further in, and allow God's light and truth to shine down onto them for revelation.

Psalm 44:5 declares, "Through You we will push down our enemies; Through Your name we will trample those who rise up against us."

Hissing

First Kings 9:8 says, "And as for this house, which is exalted, everyone who passes by it will be astonished and will hiss, and say, 'Why has the LORD done thus to this land and to this house?'" God warned His people that if they turned from Him and followed other gods, they would become an astonishment, a hissing, and a curse. Jeremiah 25:9 says,

> "Behold, I will send and take all the families of the north," says the LORD, "and Nebuchadnezzar the king of Babylon, My servant, and will bring them against this land, against its inhabitants, and against these nations all around, and will utterly destroy them, and make them an astonishment, a hissing, and perpetual desolations."

He repeated this warning in Jeremiah 25:18 and Jeremiah 29:18. In these verses, God is talking to His people. Lamentations 2:15–16 says that the enemy hissed against Jerusalem: "All who pass by clap their hands at you; they hiss and shake their heads at the daughter of Jerusalem: 'Is this the city that is called the perfection of beauty, the joy of the whole earth?' All your enemies have opened their mouth against you; they hiss and gnash their teeth."

Whatever Satan does, we can also do. Remember, Satan can only imitate God. Satan cannot create. Jeremiah 51:37 talks about hissing at the enemy: "Babylon shall become a heap, a dwelling place for jackals, an astonishment and a hissing, without an inhabitant." Job talked about hissing at a wicked man in Job 27:23: "Men shall clap their hands at him, and shall hiss him out of his place." When we hiss at the devil, we are speaking his language (the serpent's language). We are literally driving him off the stage like an audience does with a terrible performer sometimes. In Hebrew, the word for "hiss" means "to whistle or hiss (as a call or in scorn). *Webster's Dictionary* says hissing is used to show dislike or disapproval.

Keeping Silence

Ecclesiastes 3:7 says there is a time to keep silence as well as a time to speak. Shouting, clapping, and hissing are valuable and legitimate weapons of warfare for us. However, sometimes the best weapon, and the most effective, is silence. Amos 5:13 warns us that in the days of wickedness, one should keep quiet: "Therefore the prudent keep silent at that time, for it is an evil time." Proverbs 23:9 says, "Do not speak in the hearing of a fool, for he will despise the wisdom of your words." Also, Proverbs 26:4 says, "Do not answer a fool according to his folly, lest you also be like him." Sometimes the best answer is silence.

We can be snared by the words of our mouth, according to Proverbs 6:2: "You are snared by the words of your mouth; you are taken by the words of your mouth." We will be judged before God for the words we have spoken. Matthew 12:36–37 says, "But I say to you that for every idle word men may speak, they will give account of it in the day of judgment, for by your words you will be justified, and by your words you will be condemned."

There was a song in World War II about loose lips. In that song, it warned people to keep their mouths silent since "walls have ears" and spies may be listening to your conversation. The slogan was "loose lips sink ships." The Israelites were silent when marching around Jericho (Josh. 6:10). Think how unnerving that would have been. At first, the sound of the ram's horns being blown by the priests would attract people to the city walls. But to see an entire army silently marching by would be disturbing. Maybe the citizens of Jericho threw down insults, but got no response. Six days of that would get people wondering what was happening. The seventh day, they watched the army march around seven times. By that point in time, I think they just also silently watched. The roar that went up when the army shouted was startling, to say the least. It was powerful enough to bring the walls down around the city in such a way that they fell flat to enable the Israelites to go straight in.

The Lord can discern and know our thoughts. However, He doesn't judge us for our thoughts. He judges us for our words. Satan cannot read our minds. Satan is not omniscient. But he does have "spies" that eavesdrop on our conversations. Successful military campaigns, such as Israel's Operation Entebbe, the counter terrorist hostage-rescue mission at Entebbe airport in Uganda in July 1976, are due to their complete secrecy. We must remember we are in warfare. Don't give the devil any information or ammunition that he can use against you or against those you love.

Job's friends were silent (Job 2:13).
Jesus was silent
1. before the high priest (Matt. 26:62–63),
2. before Pilate (Matt. 27:14),
3. before Herod (Luke 23:9),
4. in the presence of a sinner's accusers (John 8:6).

Jesus also commanded others to be silent:
1. The leper who was cleansed (Matt. 8:4)

2. The two blind men He healed (Matt. 9:30)
3. The great multitudes He healed (Matt. 12:15–16)
4. After the transfiguration (Matt. 17:9)

God told Moses to be silent in Exodus 14:14: "The LORD will fight for you, and you shall hold your peace." God also told Job to be silent in Job 33:31: "Give ear, Job, listen to me; hold your peace, and I will speak."

Did you know that sometimes our weapons are for the benefit of others who may not know they have an issue that God wants to deal with? Gossip is a very common problem. When we refuse to get involved in those conversations, or when we refuse to answer someone who is gossiping, it starves that spirit of gossip. Our silence in those situations helps the person who is gossiping by "killing" the conversation.

Document of Confirmation

If God tells you something, write it down! Once you have recorded the word of the Lord to you, you have something to look back to, sometimes years later, to confirm the Word that God spoke to you. The written word is very important to God. He wrote His words down so we could read them centuries later. His Word still applies to lives today. He promised that not one jot or tittle would disappear until all of His Word has come to pass.

"It is written" is used often in the Bible. The word *written* is mentioned 273 times in Scripture. Jesus said, "It is written" when answering the devil's temptations at the beginning of His ministry. If Jesus used the written Word as His weapon against the enemy's tactics, don't you think we should too? When praying, we can boldly say, "It is written" and quote scripture in our prayers. God promises that His Word will not return void, but will accomplish what it was sent out to do. We send it out in faith, and God allows His will to be done.

In Exodus 34:27, God instructed Moses to write His words down because God was making a covenant with Moses and with Israel. When someone gives you a personal prophecy, write it down.

You can meditate on it, reread it, pray about it, and ask God if the word is accurate. Writing it down preserves it since we will most likely forget at least part, if not all of it because of our human nature. When written, you can reread it as often as you like and pray it into your "here and now."

Personal prophecies were recorded in the Bible:

1. Samuel's prophecy to Saul: 1 Samuel 10:1–10
2. Samuel's prophetic act to David: 1 Samuel 16:12–13
3. A prophet's prophecy to Jeroboam: 1 Kings 13:1–6
4. Elijah's prophecy to Ahab: 1 Kings 21:19, 22:38
5. Jesus's prophecy to Peter: John 21:18–19
6. Agabus's prophecy to Paul: Acts 21:11

There are many others. These personal prophecies, as well as corporate or national ones, were recorded for us to read and to understand the ways of God's dealings with His people. It also teaches us the authority of His word. Isaiah recorded a prophecy about Cyrus in Isaiah 44:28–45:6. Isaiah foretold the name of a man who would do all God's will and who would rebuild the temple in Jerusalem one hundred years before it was even destroyed. God also knows your future, your name, and your entire life's calling. He has a blueprint for every life. Personal prophecies can be weapons of warfare in that we can recall God's promises to us specifically and not lose heart or faith in the midst of waiting for the promises to manifest in our life.

Daniel understood the time to return to Jerusalem because of prophetic records in Scripture. See Daniel 9:1, Jeremiah 25:11, Isaiah 44:28–45:6. God had given the length of years that Israel would be in captivity (seventy) and the name of the man (Cyrus) who would rebuild Jerusalem. When God's people did return from captivity, they renewed their covenant with God. Nehemiah 9:38 states, "And because of all this, we make a sure covenant and write it; our leaders, our Levites, and our priests seal it."

God told Habakkuk to write the vision down. Habakkuk 2:2–3 says, "Then the LORD answered me and said: 'Write the vision and make it plain on tablets, that he may run who reads it. For the vision is yet for an appointed time; but at the end it will speak, and it will not lie. Though it tarries, wait for it; because it will surely come, it will not tarry.'" When God speaks to you, through a dream, a vision, or a prophecy, record it in a document of confirmation. You, your children, and your children's children will have proof of God's covenant relationship with you.

You can also write down for your children and grandchildren Scriptures, talents, giftedness, and other encouraging thoughts that God gives you. They can then have these to look at, pray about, and ponder for themselves. Having encouragements that span their years to date can be an effective deterrent against a wandering away from faith in God. Satan will do a lot to destroy the younger believer's walk with God. Having words of life written in a document of confirmation is powerful. When they are struggling with their faith, they can read these written words and be encouraged.

Psalm 102:18 says, "This will be written for the generation to come, that a people yet to be created may praise the LORD."

Other Weapons

Other weapons of warfare would naturally include prayer, intercession, fasting, angels, prayers of agreement (see Matthew 18:18–20), and tithing. These have been covered in other books by anointed authors, so I don't feel that I need to do more than mention them here. There are more weapons, I am sure, that we will discover as we seek God and need them for specific situations. If I counted correctly, I have listed sixteen weapons of warfare in this chapter. Isn't it marvelous that Father God has given us all these weapons to help us defeat the enemy? He has equipped us. We can be victorious! Just don't quit! He doesn't want us ignorant of the tools He provided for us. A cobbler isn't going to be successful if he just stares at all his tools, closes the door to his shop, and expects shoes to appear overnight. He needs to pick up the tools he has and get to work. God has given us tools, and He expects us to get to work too. We can't quit midway through the process. Sometimes warfare can take time, even years or decades, but we still win *if* we don't give up! That is why we can be full of faith, hope, and joy. We win!

14

We Win!

Last words are important. There are web sites that list the last words of famous people, real and fictional. There are books that list over 3,500 quotes of last words of people too. We have movies where the executioner gives the criminal time to say something with the question, "Do you have any last words?" Commercials for pizzas (tombstone frozen pizzas) were even created using this concept of last words.

If you knew that the words you were speaking were going to be your last words, what would you say? You wouldn't discuss the weather or the latest fashion. I think you would say what was most important to you. For those closest to you, you would tell them you love them. As an example, let's assume that your family was feuding among themselves. With your last words, would you tell the one side to continue fighting over the pots and pans? No, you would tell them to love each other. You would tell them you love them.

That's what Jesus did in His last words to His disciples, recorded in John 14–17. Most of His words were about love—His love for His followers, asking his followers to love Him and to love others. In fact, most of John 17 is about how much Jesus loves his followers. Jesus also, at least four separate times in this discourse, said things to give our hearts peace, warning His followers of things to come so that our hearts would not be troubled. He also promised at least three times that He would not leave us. Many other times, He promised to send us Holy Spirit to be with us. Finally, the other large chunk of His words was that Jesus and Father God are one, and we are one in Jesus and in the Father. Jesus's last words were about love, the close connection between the Triune God and believers, and comforting words to keep our hearts at peace. Jesus wants us to know who we are in Christ, and Whose we are. He wants us to have peace in all situations, knowing how much we are loved. He also wants us to continue the work He began, telling others about His love and the faith, hope, and joy that is available for them if they choose to accept the free gift of salvation also.

Peter addressed this same concept, by the guidance of Holy Spirit, to believers in 1 Peter 1:1–2, "Peter, an apostle of Jesus Christ, to the pilgrims of the Dispersion...elect according to the foreknowledge of God the Father, in sanctification of the Spirit, for obedience and sprinkling of the blood of Jesus Christ: Grace to you and peace be multiplied." We are pilgrims in this land. This is not our home; heaven is our home. We are elected by God, with His foreknowledge. He knew us before we were even formed in the womb, and yet He still chose us. He says we are elect. How does He know us? As sanctified by the Spirit. You see, God looks at the ending; He looks to the future. He does not look at our past. It is His foreknowledge that we are sanctified. He's looking at our future. Sanctification is a process, yet that is the way Father God already sees us. We are sanctified! Furthermore, we are sanctified by the Spirit for obedience.

But this great and amazing blessing doesn't just end there. In verses 3–4, it says that we are begotten again into living hope. This hope is actually alive, a living thing, a substance. It is inside of each one of us. We are also begotten again into an incorruptible inheritance that does not fade away, is not defiled, and is reserved specifically for each one of us. It is not just a general inheritance that those at the front of the line get more of, and maybe those at the back of the crowd won't find any left for them. It is an inheritance specifically for each one of us.

Furthermore, it says in 1 Peter 1:5 that we are guarded by God. We "are kept by the power of God." God Himself keeps us. Jesus confirms this too in His last prayer in front of the disciples before

His arrest: "I kept them in Your name. Those whom You gave Me I have kept… I…pray…that You should keep them from the evil one" (John 17:12, 15). This also includes us, not just the disciples because Jesus prayed for us too in John 17:20. God guards us; He keeps us.

We are to rejoice in this—the fact that we have a Father who sees us as already sanctified by the Spirit. We are to rejoice in the fact that we have been born anew. We are to rejoice that we have an inheritance. We are to rejoice that we are guarded by God's power. We are to rejoice that we have faith for salvation even as we experience trials here.

What are we to do with this incredible concept? First Peter 1:13–15 tells us. We are to gird up the loins of our minds. This means with a belt—the belt of truth. We are to re-cinch the belt (with all the weapons of our warfare that God has given us) on the loins of our minds as often as we need to, and get to work fulfilling Jesus's commands to us to obey His commandments. We are to be sober: alert, aware, awake, and available to our Commander. We are to rest—trust—our hope fully on God's grace which is brought to us. This means we do have God's grace. It *is*, not may be, not hopefully will be, but *is* brought to us by the revelation of Jesus Christ. We must be (which means we are capable of being) holy in all of our conduct.

How is any of this even possible for us? Hebrews 7:22 gives us the answer: "By so much more Jesus has become a surety of a better covenant." The only way any of what Peter encourages us to be and do in 1 Peter 1 is through Jesus Christ. Jesus is the assurance that we have a better covenant—a covenant that enables us to fulfill all that Jesus and Father God expect from us. Hebrews 7:25 tells us that Jesus is thoroughly, fully capable of completely saving us: "Therefore He is also able to save to the uttermost those who come to God through Him, since He always lives to make intercession for them." Jesus is able to save us "to the uttermost," which means entire completion of all, any, every, the whole of every believer; to conclude thoroughly the act of state, the ultimate result. There should be no doubt in your mind that you are thoroughly, totally, unequivocally saved by Jesus. He is not going to examine your life and find some microscopic speck that will disqualify you after your decision for Christ. He knew all about you, including decisions and actions you have yet to make or take, and He still sees you through your future position of sanctification by the Spirit. He loves you enough to convict you when you choose wrong or when you sin. Keep a tender heart toward Him, repent, and continue on the path with Holy Spirit as your guide. You must stay active in this life walk, but if you do, with humble heart, you will win.

To confirm this, look at Hebrews 8:6–7, 8, and 10–12, which quotes from Jeremiah 31:31–34:

> But now He has obtained a more excellent ministry, inasmuch as He is also Mediator of a better covenant, which was established on better promises... He says, *"Behold, the days are coming, says the LORD, when I will make a new covenant with the house of Israel and with the house of Judah... I will put My laws in their mind and write them on their hearts; and I will be their God, and they shall be My people...for all shall know Me, from the least of them to the greatest of them. For I will be merciful to their unrighteousness, and their sins and their lawless deeds I will remember no more."*

The teachings of the Bible are a shadow of the coming good things. We are in relationship with the Living God. We are in the will of God, as indicated by Hebrews 10:14: "For by one offering He has perfected forever those who are being sanctified." You are perfected through Jesus because you are being sanctified by the Spirit. Hebrews 10:22–25 continues,

> Let us draw near with a true heart in full assurance of faith, having our hearts sprinkled from an evil conscience and our bodies washed with pure water. Let us hold fast the confession

of our hope without wavering, for He who promised is faithful. And let us consider one another
in order to stir up love and good works…but
exhorting one another.

Remember, faith in Hebrews 11:3 comes from the invisible realm to the visible realm. What you need, trusting God's promises or His rescue, comes from the unseen or invisible to the visible realm. Faith equals trust. Noah built an ark, even though he had never seen it rain, to save his family. It took a long time to build the ark too. Noah continued to preach to the people while he built the ark. Imagine how dark the people's hearts had to have been since only Noah and his family were saved. Everyone Noah preached to must have rejected that preaching, except his family, yet Noah did not quit. I'm not sure if anyone even understood what an ark was since it had never rained before. Noah steadfastly continued doing what God asked him to do. He plodded along on the path God told him to walk and gained righteousness for his efforts. No matter how good or how tempting earthly ways are, the heavenly way is better. Hebrews 11:16 says, "But now they desire a better, that is, a heavenly country. Therefore God is not ashamed to be called their God, for He has prepared a city for them."

Trust in God parted the Red Sea, caused the walls of Jericho to fall down, saved Rahab and her family, caused three men to be safe in a fiery furnace, and one man to be safe in a lion's den overnight, among other examples. Trust in God strengthens us from weakness. We become strong in war, causing armies of the enemy to fall. Hebrews 11:34 says that people who trusted God "out of weakness were made strong, became valiant in battle, turned to flight the armies of the aliens." Some of us will receive our dead raised to life again. Some of us will refuse to give in, being tortured, knowing that we will obtain a better resurrection. No matter what comes our way, we win if we don't give up!

Sometimes we can become vulnerable to the enemy because the situation we're in seems like thick fog where we cannot even see our hand in front of us. Here's what God showed me. I got up one morning, and the fog was so thick and white that I couldn't even see the lake below me when I went onto my porch for my morning prayer time. Yet the sun was shining too. Because the sun was shining, the fog was bright white, not the usual gray of fog. It was actually fun to sit outside and enjoy being cocooned in the total bright white. By the end of my prayer time, the fog had completely disappeared, seemingly instantaneously. I asked God the lesson He was teaching me with the fog. When I cannot see clearly, God is still here (not over there, but right here!) and in charge. It was like His glory surrounded me and I could hear Him talking to me, Spirit to Spirit. He is still guiding me, even in the times when I cannot see anything and think I've lost my ability to see. Things will clear up and I will know which way to go or what to do. Just don't get discouraged in the fog. He's right there, leading you and me.

There is a praise and worship song by Chris Tomlin that I just love. The chorus says, "I know who goes before me, I know who stands behind, the God of angel armies is always by my side. The One who reigns forever, He is a friend of mine. The God of angel armies is always by my side." God wants us to know He is on our side, He loves us, and He has equipped us to follow His commands. He desires us to pray to Him to change the world for His glory, to rescue the lost and hurting from hell and bondage, to battle the enemy because the Earth belongs to the Lord, and the fullness thereof. Evict the squatter, Satan, from your life, your family, your neighborhood, your nation, and the world. God is so powerful, and our weapons of warfare are so powerful, we should be better than Marines or Special Forces. We win if we don't give up.

God showed me this in another vision I had one morning. The alarm was set to go off, but it woke me an hour earlier than it was set for. The sun was just rising as I came into the living room to pray. I saw a white cross with a hot magenta pink background with the sun in the center of the cross. The brightness of the sun was covered by a disc that was rotating incredibly fast. At first, I was looking at the cross and the rotating disc, thinking of the atomic power of the death and resurrection of Jesus. Jesus was not weak when He went to the cross—that was the greatest example of spiritual power we have. Then I saw waves radiating outward from the center sun. These waves were radiating equally in all directions at the same time, ever expanding outward like rings in water when something drops into it. I started praising God for His great power and love. Next, I noticed the lake below me. It looked blue and calm, but when two birds dipped their beaks in to drink, the water revealed a molten gold underneath the surface. The river that flows from the throne room out to the nations may be blue, but it is also liquid gold, filled with the glory of God. God really wants us to understand just how powerful He is, and how powerful we are in Him when we obey Him and use the weapons on our belt of truth.

I again understood the Lord was talking to me about this when I was flying from the west coast of Florida. I was sitting by the window, which I love because I love looking down on the Earth and thinking about the people who live below the plane. The sky on this flight was clear blue, and I was able to see light on the water and in the mangroves. I could see a perfect circle of the sun reflected upward to me. The moon symbolizes us since we reflect God's light, but we are also the sun on the Earth. We are the light of God in this world. We are to shine brightly and be the colors of the prism of light to bring God's love, peace, beauty, and joy to the world around us.

I noticed that when we passed over ground (earth, dirt), there was no reflection. There was no perfect circle of light. Only in rivers could I see the perfect circle of the sun reflected back to me. We are in the river of life. We have that river inside of us because Jesus said rivers of living water will flow out of our bellies. I wondered how I could see one circle of the sun yet the sun was shining down on everything below. Because the skies were totally clear, the light from the sun was hitting the banks of a river, as well as all the water in the river at the same time. Yet I saw a perfect circle reflection of the sun in the water. That spotlight of the sun actually appeared to be moving below me since the plane was moving and I continued to see the perfect circle of the sun in any body of water we crossed. God is always moving. He is always advancing. He is always doing a new thing. Yet He never changes. He is the same today as He was yesterday and as He will be tomorrow.

We are to be still and know that He is God. I was sitting still in the plane, but moving at the same time. Holy Spirit is the plane moving me and accomplishing His will for me and through me for those I'm destined to touch or impact. Holy Spirit accomplishes it.

The sun shines or beams down on everyone. Yet there is a special light—that perfect reflection of a perfect circle—that shines on His people all over the Earth. The plane finally moved into light clouds. It was more of a mist than full clouds that we were flying through. I still saw that orb of bright white light, even in the mist. We are a great cloud of witnesses. We have a great cloud of witnesses watching and cheering us on as we walk out the destiny they were longing for. We are not a big, heavy, towering cloud, but the light mist. Life is a vapor. We are mist—our bodies are here today and gone tomorrow. We are the temple of Holy Spirit. We contain Him. He is in us and we are in Him. He (Jesus, Father, Holy Spirit) is in and beside us. It is a twofold blessing—in and beside. He is our greatest companion.

Ask God to increase your hearing, so you can better respond to His commands as a soldier. We long to get closer to the One we love because we love Him. But how much closer can we get than having Him in us and us in Him? What we really are longing for are more experiences with God. If we ask Him for more experiences, I am confident we will experience more of Him. Look for these experiences. Be open to receiving them. Listen and ask God to talk to you. Expect Him to draw closer to you as you draw closer to Him. He loves you and desires this intimate relationship.

As I mentioned earlier in this chapter, what would you want to say if you knew these would be your last words? How would you live if you knew you only had fifteen years to live? One year? One day? Someone afraid of dying would be crying out for help. You are that help for those lost and dying, whether slowly or soon. Give them the truth about the gift of eternal life. Love is the most important thing Jesus wants us to know. Later, Jesus will come again with judgment, but right now we are still in the period of grace. Love is what draws people.

Sunlight is alive. Light is alive. Jesus is alive, and Jesus is the light of the world. The Word of God is not a book. It is the person of Jesus Christ: "In the beginning was the Word, and the Word was with God, and the Word was God" (John 1:1). "I am the way, the truth, and the life. No one comes to the Father except through Me" (John 14:6). Don't be deceived into thinking there is more than one way. Don't make the mistake of thinking that God will bend His rules for someone who was well liked, popular, a cultural icon, or just a nice person but not a believer in Christ. A good soldier knows exactly what his orders are from his commander, and he follows them exactly.

Second Peter 1:4 tells us that God has granted, or given, us promises so that through those promises we may (permission granted!) become partakers in the divine nature. That is the Word of God—the Scriptures. Those are our promises. That is the vehicle through which we become partakers of the divine nature. Hebrews 4:12 says that the Word of God is alive and active and sharper than any two-edged sword. First Samuel 13:19–22 tells the story that the Israelites could not fight effectively against the Philistines because the Philistines prevented the Israelites from having swords. The only blacksmiths were Philistines. The enemy will try to convince you that you haven't got the tools to fight him. *He is a liar!* The enemy will convince you that you are not equipped to fulfill the great commission of making disciples of the nations, raising the dead, healing the sick, casting out demons, and expanding the kingdom of heaven. The enemy is a liar!

The belt of truth is full of weapons of warfare we can wage in prayer and while walking out our lives against the plans and attacks of the enemy. There is another chorus, from the song "Thrive" by Casting Crowns, that fills my heart every time I hear it. It says, "Joy unspeakable, Faith unsinkable, Love unstoppable, anything is possible!" That is what we should be singing as our marching cadence as the army of God. He loves us so much. The song of all songs is His heartbeat of love for each one of us. He desires that we live from a position of power: of faith, hope, and joy for ourselves and to help others.

Righteousness shall be the belt of His loins,
and faithfulness the belt of His waist.

—Isaiah 11:5

INTRODUCTION
TO APPENDICES

My husband and I went to Canada for a special meeting of believers. I was so excited about going to this meeting, and I was determined to go. Nothing was going to stop me because I was sure that this particular meeting was an answer to prayers that I had been praying asking God to fill me, touch me, and take me to a higher level with Him. We decided to drive there, and visit one of our daughters on the way.

As we were almost to the Canadian border, I realized I had left our passports at home. My stomach sunk, and my heart was in a panic. My husband called our office to see if they had a copy of our passports that they could send us via email or text on our phones. They had his, but not mine. The Canadian border control personnel were wonderful. As we sat waiting to be interviewed, I continued to pray (which I started to do immediately after realizing that I left the passports!). I claimed the attendance at this meeting as a gift from God and refused to give it up to the enemy. I thanked God for the opportunity to go to this meeting since it was what I thought might be a "once in a lifetime" opportunity. The border guard let us into Canada and chuckled when I commented that the USA might not let us back in after the meeting. He said, "Oh, I'm sure they'll let you in!"

Due to the passport fiasco, and the fact that we had not realized that our destination was in the time zone 1 hour ahead of ours, we were late to the meeting. We missed the first part, but were there in time for the main portion and prayer afterward. The people at the meeting were amazed that we even were allowed into Canada, and the speaker commented about the fact that he could see that we had too much of God's glory on us to not be allowed in. I took that comment as confirmation again that this particular meeting was a part of God's destiny for me. There were confirmations later that night and the next day that confirmed the words spoken over us and that further confirmed that meeting was God's gift and plan for me to attend.

The next day, we thought to go back through the same border crossing, but missed a turn. We wound up at a larger border crossing. I wasn't worried about getting back into the USA because of all the confirmations that this was God's plan for our lives, and the "prophetic word" the Canadian border guard said on our way into Canada. So I got a bit lazy and didn't pray about it.

Our US border agent at the larger crossing must have been a former Marine Drill Sargent. He asked us over and over how we could leave our passports at home. My husband was respectfully answering the questions, admitting our mistake. This went on for enough time that I thought I'd better start praying. Duh! He refused to look at our phones to see a picture of my husband's passport (phones are not allowed to be used in that area) and asked us if we had anything like a global entry card. I said that we did, but they were also safely stored at home. My husband thought he might have them in his briefcase, but by this time the border guard was so irritated at us that we were not about to get out of the car to rummage through the briefcase without his permission.

He asked again how stupid could we be to forget the passports. I finally spoke up before my husband could and said I made a mistake and totally forgot them since I was packing for us both. He then took our driver's licenses and closed the window of his station on us. Just as I finished silently praying, he opened the window and let us through. Back on US soil! With the border guard's attitude toward us, it was a bit of a harrowing experience.

When we got home, it turns out that my husband did have the global entry cards in his briefcase, which I thought were safely tucked away at home. I couldn't believe he had them in his briefcase! We could have saved ourselves two hours of "interview" time, and stress, and made the trip a whole lot easier if we'd had them out and ready to show both ways.

I asked God what He was trying to show me in this situation, and just laughed at His answer. This border entry fiasco was a life example of the purpose for this book. It was a picture of a lot of believers—we have the right tools with us, but fail to realize they are there for us to use. We fail to realize we even have them with us, or we fail to realize they even exist for us to use. I knew I had the passports and the global entry cards, but failed to carry them with us to pull them out when needed. Being safely tucked away at home, they were totally useless to us when we needed them. We may carry our Bible with us, but we need to dig a little and realize that God has given us every tool we need, and then pull these tools out as needed and use them!

I hope this story gives you as vivid a picture as God gave me of what happens to us as children of God when we fail to use the weapons and authority God has given us. Our lives are more stressed, time is wasted, and maybe, spiritually, roads we intended to travel on are blocked.

I have put together the following appendixes so that you could meditate on the Scripture lists I compiled over the years, and learn for yourself what God wants you to know from these Scriptures. I also included a sample prayer for the baptism of Holy Spirit, but I want you to realize your prayer is just conversation with your Father in heaven. Use your own wording if desired.

APPENDIX A

THE POWER OF THE WORD OF GOD

Listed below are just some of the Scriptures (NKJV unless otherwise noted) that depict the power of God's Word. Read these and let His Word strengthen and encourage your heart. Use them to defeat your enemies and take back territory for our king.

Genesis 1:3: "Then God said...and there was..."

Genesis 1:6–7: "Then God said... Thus God made..."

Genesis 1:9: "Then God said...and it was so."

Genesis 1:11: "Then God said...and it was so."

Genesis 1:14–15: "Then God said...and it was so."

Genesis 1:20–21: "Then God said... So God created..."

Genesis 1:24: "Then God said...and it was so."

Genesis 1:26–27: "Then God said... So God created..."

Genesis 18:10: "And He said, 'I will certainly return to you according to the time of life, and behold, Sarah your wife shall have a son.'"

Genesis 21:1 and 2: "And the LORD visited Sarah as He had said, and the LORD did for Sarah as He had spoken. For Sarah conceived and bore Abraham a son in his old age, at the set time of which God had spoken to him."

Exodus 34:27: "Then the LORD said to Moses, 'Write these words, for according to the tenor of these words I have made a covenant with you and with Israel.'"

Deuteronomy 8:3: "So He humbled you, allowed you to hunger, and fed you with manna which you did not know nor did your fathers know, that He might make you know that man shall not live by bread alone; but man lives by every word that proceeds from the mouth of the LORD."

Deuteronomy 18:18: "I will raise up for them a Prophet like you from among their brethren, and will put My words in His mouth, and He shall speak to them all that I command Him."

Deuteronomy 32:46–47: "And he said to them: 'Set your hearts on all the words which I testify among you today, which you shall command your children to be careful to observe: all the words of this law. For it is not a futile thing for you, because it is your life, and by this word you shall prolong your days in the land which you cross over the Jordan to possess.'"

2 Kings 22:11, 13: "Now it happened, when the king heard the words of the Book of the Law, that he tore his clothes...'Go, inquire of the LORD for me, for the people and for all Judah, concerning the words of this book that has been found; for great is the wrath of the LORD that is aroused against us, because our fathers have not obeyed the words of this book, to do according to all that is written concerning us.'"

Psalm 119:81: "My soul faints for Your salvation, but I hope in Your word."

Psalm 119:89: "Forever, O LORD, Your word is settled in heaven."

Psalm 119:101: "I have restrained my feet from every evil way, that I may keep Your word."

Psalm 119:105: "Your word is a lamp to my feet and a light to my path."

Psalm 119:114: "You are my hiding place and my shield; I hope in Your word."

Psalm 119:116: "Uphold me according to Your word, that I may live; and do not let me be ashamed of my hope."

Psalm 119:130: "The entrance of Your words gives light; It gives understanding to the simple."

Psalm 119:154: "Plead my cause and redeem me; Revive me according to Your word."

Psalm 119:160: "The entirety of Your word is truth, and every one of Your righteous judgments endures forever."

Psalm 119:162: "I rejoice at Your word as one who finds great treasure."

Psalm 138:2: "I will worship toward Your holy temple, and praise Your name for Your lovingkindness and Your truth; For You have magnified Your word above all Your name."

Psalm 148:5–6: "Let them praise the name of the LORD, for He commanded and they were created. He also established them forever and ever; He made a decree which shall not pass away."

Proverbs 2:6: "For the LORD gives wisdom; from His mouth come knowledge and understanding."

Proverbs 30:5–6: "Every word of God is pure; He is a shield to those who put their trust in Him. Do not add to His words, lest He rebuke you, and you be found a liar."

Isaiah 44:8: "Do not fear, nor be afraid; Have I not told you from that time, and declared it? You are My witnesses. Is there a God besides Me? Indeed there is no other Rock; I know not one."

Isaiah 45:22–23: "Look to Me, and be saved, all you ends of the earth! For I am God, and there is no other. I have sworn by Myself; the word has gone out of My mouth in righteousness, and shall not return, that to Me every knee shall bow, every tongue shall take an oath."

Isaiah 46:9–11: "Remember the former things of old, for I am God, and there is no other; I am God, and there is none like Me, declaring the end from the beginning, and from ancient times things that are not yet done, saying, 'My counsel shall stand, and I will do all My pleasure…' Indeed I have spoken it; I will also bring it to pass. I have purposed it; I will also do it."

Isaiah 55:11: "So shall My word be that goes forth from My mouth; It shall not return to Me void, but it shall accomplish what I please, and it shall prosper in the thing for which I sent it."

Isaiah 59:21: "'As for Me,' says the LORD, 'this is My covenant with them: My Spirit who is upon you, and My words which I have put in your mouth, shall not depart from your mouth, nor from the mouth of your descendants, nor from the mouth of your descendants' descendants,' says the LORD, 'from this time and forevermore.'"

Jeremiah 1:12: "Then the LORD said to me, 'You have seen well, for I am ready to perform My word.'"

Jeremiah 5:14: "Therefore thus says the LORD God of hosts: 'Because you speak this word, behold, I will make My words in your mouth fire, and this people wood, and it shall devour them.'"

Jeremiah 15:16: "Your words were found, and I ate them, and Your word was to me the joy and rejoicing of my heart; for I am called by Your name, O LORD God of hosts."

Jeremiah 23:29: "'Is not My word like a fire?' says the LORD, 'And like a hammer that breaks the rock in pieces?'"

Lamentations 2:17a: "The LORD has done what He purposed; He has fulfilled His word which He commanded in days of old."

Ezekiel 2:7: "You shall speak My words to them, whether they hear or whether they refuse, for they are rebellious."

Ezekiel 12:28: "Therefore say to them, 'Thus says the LORD GOD: "None of My words will be postponed any more, but the word which I speak will be done," says the LORD GOD.'"

Matthew 4:4: "But He answered and said, 'It is written, "Man shall not live by bread alone, but by every word that proceeds from the mouth of God."'"

Matthew 24:35: "Heaven and earth will pass away, but My words will by no means pass away."

Luke 1:37: "For with God nothing will be impossible."

John 1:1, 4: "In the beginning was the Word, and the Word was with God, and the Word was God... In Him was life, and the life was the light of men."

John 3:34: "For He whom God has sent speaks the words of God, for God does not give the Spirit by measure."

John 4:41: "And many more believed because of His own word."

John 5:24: "Most assuredly, I say to you, he who hears My word and believes in Him who sent Me has everlasting life, and shall not come into judgment, but has passed from death into life."

John 6:63: "It is the Spirit who gives life; the flesh profits nothing. The words that I speak to you are spirit, and they are life."

John 6:68: "But Simon Peter answered Him, 'Lord, to whom shall we go? You have the words of eternal life.'"

John 8:47a: "He who is of God hears God's words…"

John 8:51: "Most assuredly, I say to you, if anyone keeps my word he shall never see death."

John 12:49–50: "For I have not spoken on My own authority, but the Father who sent Me gave Me a command, what I should say and what I should speak. And I know that His command is everlasting life. Therefore, whatever I speak, just as the Father has told Me, so I speak."

John 15:3: "You are already clean because of the word which I have spoken to you."

John 15:7: "If you abide in Me, and My words abide in you, you will ask what you desire, and it shall be done for you."

John 15:11: "These things I have spoken to you, that My joy may remain in you, and that your joy may be full."

John 16:13: "However, when He, the Spirit of truth, has come, He will guide you into all truth; for He will not speak on His own authority, but whatever He hears He will speak; and He will tell you things to come."

John 17:6, 8: "I have manifested Your name to the men whom You have given Me out of the world. They were Yours, You gave them to Me, and they have kept Your word… For I have given to them the words which You have given Me; and they have received them, and have known surely that I came forth from You; and they have believed that You sent me."

Romans 10:17: "So then faith comes by hearing, and hearing by the word of God."

1 Corinthians 4:20: "For the kingdom of God is not in word but in power."

Ephesians 6:17: "And take the helmet of salvation, and the sword of the Spirit, which is the word of God."

1 Thessalonians 1:5: "For our gospel did not come to you in word only, but also in power, and in the Holy Spirit and in much

assurance, as you know what kind of men we were among you for your sake."

2 Timothy 2:9: "For which I suffer trouble as an evildoer, even to the point of chains, but the word of God is not chained."

Hebrews 4:12: "For the word of God is living and powerful, and sharper than any two-edged sword, piercing even to the division of soul and spirit, and of joints and marrow, and is a discerner of the thoughts and intents of the heart."

1 Peter 1:23–25: "having been born again, not of corruptible seed but incorruptible, through the word of God which lives and abides forever, because *'All flesh is as grass, and all the glory of man as the flower of the grass. The grass withers, and its flower falls away, but the word of the* LORD *endures forever.'"*

2 Peter 1:19: "And so we have the prophetic word confirmed, which you do well to heed as a light that shines in a dark place, until the day dawns and the morning star rises in your hearts."

2 Peter 3:8–9: "But, beloved, do not forget this one thing, that with the LORD one day is as a thousand years, and a thousand years as one day. The Lord is not slack concerning His promise, as some count slackness, but is longsuffering toward us, not willing that any should perish, but that all should come to repentance."

1 John 2:5: "But whoever keeps His word, truly the love of God is perfected in him. By this we know that we are in Him."

1 John 2:14b: "I have written to you, young men, because you are strong, and the word of God abides in you, and you have overcome the wicked one."

Revelation 1:13–14, 16: "and in the midst of the seven lampstands One like the Son of Man, clothed with a garment down to the feet and girded about the chest with a golden band. His head and hair were white like wool, as white as snow, and His eyes like a flame of fire;... He had in His right hand seven stars, out of His mouth went a sharp two-edged sword, and His countenance was like the sun shining in its strength."

Revelation 2:12, 16: "And to the angel of the church in Pergamos write, 'These things says He who has the sharp two-edged sword...

Repent, or else I will come to you quickly and will fight against them with the sword of My mouth.'"

Revelation 21:5: "Then He who sat on the throne said, 'Behold, I make all things new.' And He said to me, 'Write, for these words are true and faithful.'"

APPENDIX B

CHRIST'S AUTHORITY
GIVEN TO BELIEVERS

Listed below are just some of the Scriptures that show us the authority and power available to us as believers. Read these and let His word strengthen and encourage your heart. Meditate on these Scriptures so His truth sinks in and becomes the strength in your intercessor-warrior's heart.

Deuteronomy 28:13: "And the LORD will make you the head and not the tail; you shall be above only, and not be beneath, if you heed the commandments of the LORD your God, which I command you today, and are careful to observe them."

Matthew 16:19: "And I will give you the keys of the kingdom of heaven, and whatever you bind on earth will be bound in heaven and whatever you loose on earth will be loosed in heaven."

Matthew 28:18–20: "And Jesus came and spoke to them, saying, 'All authority has been given to Me in heaven and on earth. Go therefore and make disciples of all the nations, baptizing them in the name of the Father and of the Son and of the Holy Spirit, teaching them to observe all things that I have commanded you; and lo, I am with you always, even to the end of the age.'"

Mark 6:7, 13: "And He called the twelve to Himself, and began to send them out two by two, and gave them power over unclean spirits... And they cast out many demons, and anointed with oil many who were sick, and healed them."

Mark 16:15–18: "And He said to them, 'Go into all the world and preach the gospel to every creature. He who believes and is baptized will be saved; but he who does not believe will be condemned. And these signs will follow those who believe: In My name they will cast out demons; they will speak with new tongues; they will take up serpents; and if they drink anything deadly, it will by no means hurt them; they will lay hands on the sick, and they will recover."

Luke 9:1–2: "Then He called His twelve disciples together and gave them power and authority over all demons, and to cure diseases. He sent them to preach the kingdom of God and to heal the sick."

Luke 10:16: "He who hears you hears Me, he who rejects you rejects Me, and he who rejects Me rejects Him who sent Me."

Luke 10:17: "Then the seventy returned with joy, saying, 'Lord, even the demons are subject to us in Your name.'"

Luke 10:19: "Behold, I give you the authority to trample on serpents and scorpions, and over all the power of the enemy, and nothing shall by any means hurt you."

John 14:12–14: "Most assuredly, I say to you, he who believes in Me, the works that I do he will do also; and greater works than these he will do, because I go to My Father. And whatever you ask in My name, that I will do, that the Father may be glorified in the Son. If you ask anything in My name, I will do it."

John 14:20: "At that day you will know that I am in My Father, and you in Me, and I in you."

John 15:16: "You did not choose Me, but I chose you and appointed you that you should go and bear fruit, and that your fruit should remain, that whatever you ask the Father in My name He may give you."

John 16:13–15: "However, when He, the Spirit of truth, has come, He will guide you into all truth; for He will not speak on His own authority, but whatever He hears He will speak; and He will tell you things to come. He will glorify Me, for He will take of what is Mine and declare it to you. All things that the Father has are Mine. Therefore I said that He will take of Mine and declare it to you."

John 16:23–24: "And in that day you will ask Me nothing. Most assuredly, I say to you, whatever you ask the Father in My name He will give you. Until now you have asked nothing in My name. Ask, and you will receive, that your joy may be full."

John 17:16–19: "They are not of the world, just as I am not of the world. Sanctify them by Your truth. Your word is truth. As you sent Me into the world, I also have sent them into the world. And for their sakes I sanctify Myself, that they also may be sanctified by the truth."

John 17:20–23: "I do not pray for these alone, but also for those who will believe in Me through their word; that they all may be one, as You, Father, are in Me, and I in You; that they also may be one in Us, that the world may believe that You sent Me. And the glory which You gave Me I have given them, that they may be one just as We are one: I in them, and You in Me; that they may be made perfect in one, and that the world may know that You have sent Me, and have loved them as You have loved Me."

John 17:26: "And I have declared to them Your name, and will declare it, that the love with which You loved Me may be in them, and I in them."

John 20:21–22: "So Jesus said to them again, 'Peace to you! As the Father has sent Me, I also send you.' And when He had said this, He breathed on them, and said to them, 'Receive the Holy Spirit.'"

Acts 2:38–39: "Then Peter said to them, 'Repent, and let every one of you be baptized in the name of Jesus Christ for the remission of sins; and you shall receive the gift of the Holy Spirit. For the promise is to you and to your children, and to all who are afar off, as many as the Lord our God will call.'"

Acts 2:43: "Then fear came upon every soul, and many wonders and signs were done through the apostles."

Acts 3:6–8: "Then Peter said, 'Silver and gold I do not have, but what I do have I give you: In the name of Jesus Christ of Nazareth, rise up and walk.' And he took him by the right hand and lifted him up, and immediately his feet and ankle bones received strength. So he, leaping up, stood and walked and entered the temple with them: walking, leaping, and praising God."

Acts 3:12, 16: "So when Peter saw it, he responded to the people: 'Men of Israel, why do you marvel at this? Or why look so intently at us, as though by our own power or godliness we had made this man walk... And His name, through faith in His name, has made this man strong, whom you see and know. Yes, the faith which comes through Him has given him this perfect soundness in the presence of you all."

Acts 4:29–31: "Now, Lord, look on their threats, and grant to Your servants that with all boldness they may speak Your word, by stretching out Your hand to heal, and that signs and wonders may be done through the name of Your holy Servant Jesus."

Acts 16:17–18: "This girl followed Paul and us, and cried out, saying, 'These men are the servants of the Most High God, who proclaim to us the way of salvation.' And this she did for many days. But Paul, greatly annoyed, turned and said to the spirit, 'I command you in the name of Jesus Christ to come out of her.' And he came out that very hour."

Romans 1:5–6: "Through Him we have received grace and apostleship for obedience to the faith among all nations for His name, among whom you also are the called of Jesus Christ."

2 Corinthians 2:14: "Now thanks be to God who always leads us in triumph in Christ, and through us diffuses the fragrance of His knowledge in every place."

2 Corinthians 3:4–6: "And we have such trust through Christ toward God. Not that we are sufficient of ourselves to think of any-thing as being from ourselves, but our sufficiency is from God, who also made us sufficient as ministers of the new covenant, not of the letter but of the Spirit; for the letter kills, but the Spirit gives life."

2 Corinthians 3:12: "Therefore, since we have such hope, we use great boldness of speech."

2 Corinthians 3:18: But we all, with unveiled face, beholding as in a mirror the glory of the Lord, are being transformed into the same image from glory to glory, just as by the Spirit of the Lord."

2 Corinthians 4:6: "For it is the God who commanded light to shine out of darkness, who has shone in our hearts to give the light of the knowledge of the glory of God in the face of Jesus Christ."

Ephesians 2:4–6: "But God, who is rich in mercy, because of His great love with which He loved us, even when we were dead in trespasses, made us alive together with Christ (by grace you have been saved), and raised us up together, and made us sit together in the heavenly places in Christ Jesus."

Ephesians 6:10–11, 16: "Finally, my brethren, be strong in the Lord and in the power of His might. Put on the whole armor of God, that you may be able to stand against the wiles of the devil...above all, taking the shield of faith with which you will be able to quench all the fiery darts of the wicked one."

Colossians 2:6–7: "As you therefore have received Christ Jesus the Lord, so walk in Him, rooted and built up in Him and estab-lished in the faith, as you have been taught, abounding in it with thanksgiving."

Colossians 2:10: "and you are complete in Him, who is the head of all principality and power."

Colossians 3:12–14: "Therefore, as the elect of God, holy and beloved, put on tender mercies, kindness, humility, meekness, long-suffering; bearing with one another, and forgiving one another, if anyone has a complaint against another; even as Christ forgave you, so you also must do."

Colossians 3:17: "And whatever you do in word or deed, do all in the name of the Lord Jesus, giving thanks to God the Father through Him."

Titus 2:15: "Speak these things, exhort, and rebuke with all authority. Let no one despise you."

James 4:7: "Therefore submit to God. Resist the devil and he will flee from you."

James 5:15–16: "And the prayer of faith will save the sick, and the Lord will raise him up. And if he has committed sins, he will be forgiven. Confess your trespasses to one another, and pray for one another, that you may be healed. The effective, fervent prayer of a righteous man avails much."

James 5:20: "Let him know that he who turns a sinner from the error of his way will save a soul from death and cover a multitude of sins."

2 Peter 1:2–4: "Grace and peace be multiplied to you in the knowledge of God and of Jesus our Lord, as His divine power has given to us all things that pertain to life and godliness, through the knowledge of Him who called us by glory and virtue, by which have been given to us exceedingly great and precious promises, that through these you may be partakers of the divine nature, having escaped the corruption that is in the world through lust."

1 John 5:4: "For whatever is born of God overcomes the world. And this is the victory that has overcome the world: our faith."

1 John 5:11–12: "And this is the testimony: that God has given us eternal life, and this life is in His Son. He who has the Son has life; he who does not have the Son of God does not have life."

Revelation 2:26–27: "And he who overcomes, and keeps My works until the end, to him I will give power over the nations...as I also have received from My Father."

APPENDIX C

Scriptures to Prepare You to Pray

Listed below are just some of the Scriptures that will help you come into the place of faith and readiness so that your prayers can be truly powerful and effective. Read these and let His Word strengthen and encourage your heart.

Exodus 15:1–3: "Then Moses and the children of Israel sang this song to the Lord, and spoke, saying: 'I will sing to the Lord, For He has triumphed gloriously! The horse and its rider He has thrown into the sea! The Lord is my strength and song, and He has become my salvation; He is my God, and I will praise Him; My father's God, and I will exalt Him. The Lord is a man of war; the Lord is His name."

2 Kings 6:15–17: "And when the servant of the man of God arose early and went out, there was an army, surrounding the city with horses and chariots. And his servant said to him, 'Alas, my master! What shall we do?' So he answered, 'Do not fear, for those who are with us are more than those who are with them.' And Elisha prayed, and said, 'Lord, I pray, open his eyes that he may see.' Then the Lord opened the eyes of the young man, and he saw. And behold, the mountain was full of horses and chariots of fire all around Elisha."

2 Chronicles 20:3, 6, 11–12, 15b, 17: "And Jehoshaphat feared, and set himself to seek the Lord, and proclaimed a fast throughout all Judah…and said, 'O Lord God of our fathers, are You not God in heaven, and do You not rule over all the kingdoms of the nations,

and in Your hand is there not power and might, so that no one is able to withstand You?... Here they are, rewarding us by coming to throw us out of Your possession which You have given us to inherit. O our God, will You not judge them? For we have no power against this great multitude that is coming against us; nor do we know what to do, but our eyes are upon You.' Thus says the LORD to you: 'Do not be afraid nor dismayed because of this great multitude, for the battle is not yours, but God's... You will not need to fight in this battle. Position yourselves, stand still and see the salvation of the LORD, who is with you, O Judah and Jerusalem!' Do not fear or be dismayed; tomorrow go out against them, for the LORD is with you."

Esther 4:14: "For if you remain completely silent at this time, relief and deliverance will arise for the Jews from another place, but you and your father's house will perish. Yet who knows whether you have come to the kingdom for such a time as this?"

Job 42:1, 2, 5: "Then Job answered the LORD and said: 'I know that You can do everything, and that no purpose of Yours can be withheld from You... I have heard of You by the hearing of the ear, but now my eye sees You."

Psalm 17:6–9: "I have called upon You, for You will hear me, O God; incline Your ear to me, and hear my speech. Show Your marvelous lovingkindness by Your right hand, O You who save those who trust in You from those who rise up against them. Keep me as the apple of Your eye; Hide me under the shadow of Your wings, from the wicked who oppress me, from my deadly enemies who surround me."

Psalm 19:14: "Let the words of my mouth and the meditation of my heart be acceptable in Your sight, O LORD, my strength and my Redeemer."

Psalm 27:1, 13–14: "The LORD is my light and my salvation; whom shall I fear? The LORD is the strength of my life; of whom shall I be afraid?... I would have lost heart, unless I had believed that I would see the goodness of the LORD in the land of the living. Wait on the LORD; Be of good courage, and He shall strengthen your heart; Wait, I say, on the LORD!"

Psalm 56:10–11, 13: "In God (I will praise His word), In the LORD (I will praise His word), In God I have put my trust; I will not be afraid. What can man do to me?… For You have delivered my soul from death. Have You not kept my feet from falling, that I may walk before God in the light of the living?"

Psalm 57:1–3: "Be merciful to me, O God, be merciful to me! For my soul trusts in You; And in the shadow of Your wings I will make my refuge, until these calamities have passed by. I will cry out to God Most High, to God who performs all things for me. He shall send from heaven and save me; He reproaches the one who would swallow me up. Selah God shall send forth His mercy and His truth."

Psalm 85:7–13: "Show us Your mercy, LORD, and grant us Your salvation. I will hear what God the LORD will speak, for He will speak peace to His people and to His saints; but let them not turn back to folly. Surely His salvation is near to those who fear Him, that glory may dwell in our land. Mercy and truth have met together; Righteousness and peace have kissed. Truth shall spring out of the earth, and righteousness shall look down from heaven. Yes, the LORD will give what is good; and our land will yield its increase. Righteousness will go before Him, and shall make His footsteps our pathway."

Psalm 91:1–6: "He who dwells in the secret place of the Most High shall abide under the shadow of the Almighty. I will say of the LORD, 'He is my refuge and my fortress; My God, in Him I will trust.' Surely He shall deliver you from the snare of the fowler and from the perilous pestilence. He shall cover you with His feathers, and under His wings you shall take refuge. His truth shall be your shield and buckler. You shall not be afraid of the terror by night, nor of the arrow that flies by day, nor of the pestilence that walks in darkness, nor of the destruction that lays waste at noonday."

Psalm 91:9–11: "Because you have made the LORD, who is my refuge, even the Most High, your dwelling place, no evil shall befall you, nor shall any plague come near your dwelling; for He shall give His angels charge over you, to keep you in all your ways."

Psalm 91:14–16: "Because he has set his love upon Me, therefore I will deliver him; I will set him on high, because he has known

My name. He shall call upon Me, and I will answer him; I will be with him in trouble; I will deliver him and honor him. With long life I will satisfy him, and show him My salvation."

Psalm 96:2–4: "Sing to the LORD, bless His name; Proclaim the good news of His salvation from day to day. Declare His glory among the nations, His wonders among all peoples. For the LORD is great and greatly to be praised; He is to be feared above all gods."

Psalm 118:6–9: "The LORD is on my side; I will not fear. What can man do to me? The LORD is for me among those who help me; Therefore I shall see my desire on those who hate me. It is better to trust in the LORD than to put confidence in man. It is better to trust in the LORD than to put confidence in princes."

Isaiah 35:3–6: "Strengthen the weak hands, and make firm the feeble knees. Say to those who are fearful-hearted, 'Be strong, do not fear! Behold, your God will come with vengeance, with the recompense of God; He will come and save you.' Then the eyes of the blind shall be opened, and the ears of the deaf shall be unstopped. Then the lame shall leap like a deer, and the tongue of the dumb sing. For waters shall burst forth in the wilderness, and streams in the desert."

Isaiah 41:9–10: "You whom I have taken from the ends of the earth, and called from its farthest regions, and said to you, 'You are My servant, I have chosen you and have not cast you away: Fear not, for I am with you; Be not dismayed, for I am your God. I will strengthen you, Yes, I will help you, I will uphold you with My righteous right hand.'"

Isaiah 41:13: "For I, the LORD your God, will hold your right hand, saying to you, 'Fear not, I will help you.'"

Isaiah 43:1–4a: "But now, thus says the LORD, who created you, O Jacob, and He who formed you, O Israel: 'Fear not, for I have redeemed you; I have called you by your name; You are Mine. When you pass through the waters, I will be with you; and through the rivers, they shall not overflow you. When you walk through the fire, you shall not be burned, nor shall the flame scorch you. For I am the LORD your God, the Holy One of Israel, your Savior; I gave Egypt for your ransom, Ethiopia and Seba in your place. Since you were precious in My sight, you have been honored, and I have loved you."

Isaiah 54:4–5: "Do not fear, for you will not be ashamed; Neither be disgraced, for you will not be put to shame; for you will forget the shame of your youth, and will not remember the reproach of your widowhood anymore. For your Maker is your husband, the LORD of hosts is His name; and your Redeemer is the Holy One of Israel; He is called the God of the whole earth."

Isaiah 54:14–15: "In righteousness you shall be established; you shall be far from oppression, for you shall not fear; and from terror, for it shall not come near you. Indeed they shall surely assemble, but not because of Me. Whoever assembles against you shall fall for your sake."

Isaiah 54:17: "'No weapon formed against you shall prosper, and every tongue which rises against you in judgment you shall condemn. This is the heritage of the servants of the LORD, and their righteousness is from Me,' says the LORD."

Isaiah 60:1–2: "Arise, shine; for your light has come! And the glory of the LORD is risen upon you. For behold, the darkness shall cover the earth, and deep darkness the people; but the LORD will arise over you, and His glory will be seen upon you."

Isaiah 61:1–3: "The Spirit of the Lord GOD is upon Me, because the LORD has anointed Me to preach good tidings to the poor; He has sent Me to heal the brokenhearted, to proclaim liberty to the captives, and the opening of the prison to those who are bound; to proclaim the acceptable year of the LORD, and the day of vengeance of our God; to comfort all who mourn, to console those who mourn in Zion, to give them beauty for ashes, the oil of joy for mourning, the garment of praise for the spirit of heaviness; that they may be called trees of righteousness, the planting of the LORD, that He may be glorified."

Isaiah 62:1: "For Zion's sake I will not hold My peace, and for Jerusalem's sake I will not rest, until her righteousness goes forth as brightness, and her salvation as a lamp that burns."

Isaiah 62:6–7: "I have set watchmen on your walls, O Jerusalem; They shall never hold their peace day or night. You who make mention of the LORD, do not keep silent, and give Him no rest till He establishes and till He makes Jerusalem a praise in the earth."

Jeremiah 46:3: "Order the buckler and shield, and draw near to battle!"

Joel 3:9: "Proclaim this among the nations: 'Prepare for war! Wake up the mighty men, let all the men of war draw near, Let them come up."

Zechariah 4:6: "So he answered and said to me: 'This is the word of the LORD to Zerubbabel: "Not by might nor by power, but by My Spirit," says the LORD of hosts.'"

Mark 14:38: "Watch and pray, lest you enter into temptation. The spirit indeed is willing, but the flesh is weak."

Luke 12:4–5: "And I say to you, My friends, do not be afraid of those who kill the body, and after that have no more that they can do. But I will show you whom you should fear: Fear Him who, after He has killed, has power to cast into hell; yes, I say to you, fear Him!"

Luke 18:1: "Then He spoke a parable to them, that men always ought to pray and not lose heart."

Luke 22:46: "Then He said to them, 'Why do you sleep? Rise and pray, lest you enter into temptation.'"

John 14:12–14: "Most assuredly, I say to you, he who believes in Me, the works that I do he will do also; and greater works than these he will do, because I go to My Father. And whatever you ask in My name, that I will do, that the Father may be glorified in the Son. If you ask anything in My name, I will do it."

John 14:27: "Peace I leave with you, My peace I give to you; not as the world gives do I give to you. Let not your heart be troubled, neither let it be afraid."

John 20:21: "So Jesus said to them again, 'Peace to you! As the Father has sent Me, I also send you.'"

Acts 1:8: "But you shall receive power when the Holy Spirit has come upon you; and you shall be witnesses to Me in Jerusalem, and in all Judea and Samaria, and to the end of the earth."

Romans 8:35, 37: "Who shall separate us from the love of Christ? Shall tribulation, or distress, or persecution, or famine, or nakedness, or peril, or sword?... Yet in all these things we are more than conquerors through Him who loved us."

Romans 13:10–14: "Love does no harm to a neighbor; therefore love is the fulfillment of the law. And do this, knowing the time, that now it is high time to awake out of sleep; for now our salvation is nearer than when we first believed. The night is far spent, the day is at hand. Therefore let us cast off the works of darkness, and let us put on the armor of light. Let us walk properly, as in the day, not in revelry and drunkenness, not in lewdness and lust, not in strife and envy. But put on the Lord Jesus Christ, and make no provision for the flesh, to fulfill its lusts."

2 Corinthians 10:3–5: "For though we walk in the flesh, we do not war according to the flesh. For the weapons of our warfare are not carnal but mighty in God for pulling down strongholds, casting down arguments and every high thing that exalts itself against the knowledge of God, bringing every thought into captivity to the obedience of Christ."

Galatians 3:26–29: "For you are all sons of God through faith in Christ Jesus. For as many of you as were baptized into Christ have put on Christ. There is neither Jew nor Greek, there is neither slave nor free, there is neither male nor female; for you are all one in Christ Jesus. And if you are Christ's, then you are Abraham's seed, and heirs according to the promise."

Galatians 5:1: "Stand fast therefore in the liberty by which Christ has made us free, and do not be entangled again with a yoke of bondage."

Ephesians 5:8: "For you were once darkness, but now you are light in the Lord. Walk as children of light."

Ephesians 5:13–14: "But all things that are exposed are made manifest by the light, for whatever makes manifest is light. Therefore He says: 'Awake, you who sleep, Arise from the dead, and Christ will give you light.'"

Ephesians 5:15–17: "See then that you walk circumspectly, not as fools but as wise, redeeming the time, because the days are evil. Therefore do not be unwise, but understand what the will of the Lord is."

Ephesians 6:10: "Finally, my brethren, be strong in the Lord and in the power of His might."

Philippians 4:4–9: "Rejoice in the Lord always. Again I will say, rejoice! Let your gentleness be known to all men. The Lord is at hand. Be anxious for nothing, but in everything by prayer and supplication, with thanksgiving, let your requests be made known to God; and the peace of God, which surpasses all understanding, will guard your hearts and minds through Christ Jesus. Finally, brethren, whatever things are true, whatever things are noble, whatever things are just, whatever things are pure, whatever things are lovely, whatever things are of good report, if there is any virtue and if there is anything praiseworthy: meditate on these things. The things which you learned and received and heard and saw in me, these do, and the God of peace will be with you."

Philippians 4:13: "I can do all things through Christ who strengthens me."

Colossians 1:9–12: "For this reason we also, since the day we heard it, do not cease to pray for you, and to ask that you may be filled with the knowledge of His will in all wisdom and spiritual understanding; that you may walk worthy of the Lord, fully pleasing Him, being fruitful in every good work and increasing in the knowledge of God; strengthened with all might, according to His glorious power, for all patience and longsuffering with joy; giving thanks to the Father who has qualified us to be partakers of the inheritance of the saints in the light."

Colossians 4:2: "Continue earnestly in prayer, being vigilant in it with thanksgiving."

1 Timothy 2:1–5: "Therefore I exhort first of all that supplications, prayers, intercessions, and giving of thanks be made for all men, for kings and all who are in authority, that we may lead a quiet and peaceable life in all godliness and reverence. For this is good and acceptable in the sight of God our Savior, who desires all men to be saved and to come to the knowledge of the truth. For there is one God and one Mediator between God and men, the Man Christ Jesus."

1 Timothy 6:12: "Fight the good fight of faith, lay hold on eternal life, to which you were also called and have confessed the good confession in the presence of many witnesses."

2 Timothy 2:1: "You therefore, my son, be strong in the grace that is in Christ Jesus."

2 Timothy 2:3–4: "You therefore must endure hardship as a good soldier of Jesus Christ. No one engaged in warfare entangles himself with the affairs of this life, that he may please him who enlisted him as a soldier."

Titus 2:11–15: "For the grace of God that brings salvation has appeared to all men, teaching us that, denying ungodliness and worldly lusts, we should live soberly, righteously, and godly in the present age, looking for the blessed hope and glorious appearing of our great God and Savior Jesus Christ, who gave Himself for us, that He might redeem us from every lawless deed and purify for Himself His own special people, zealous for good works. Speak these things, exhort, and rebuke with all authority. Let no one despise you."

Hebrews 12:1–3: "Therefore we also, since we are surrounded by so great a cloud of witnesses, let us lay aside every weight, and the sin which so easily ensnares us, and let us run with endurance the race that is set before us, looking unto Jesus, the author and finisher of our faith, who for the joy that was set before Him endured the cross, despising the shame, and has sat down at the right hand of the throne of God. For consider Him who endured such hostility from sinners against Himself, lest you become weary and discouraged in your souls."

Hebrews 13:5–6: "Let your conduct be without covetousness; be content with such things as you have. For He Himself has said, 'I will never leave you nor forsake you.' So we may boldly say: 'The LORD is my helper; I will not fear. What can man do to me?'"

1 Peter 1:13–16: "Therefore gird up the loins of your mind, be sober, and rest your hope fully upon the grace that is to be brought to you at the revelation of Jesus Christ; as obedient children, not conforming yourselves to the former lusts, as in your ignorance; but as He who called you is holy, you also be holy in all your conduct, because it is written, 'Be holy, for I am holy.'"

1 Peter 2:9–10: "But you are a chosen generation, a royal priesthood, a holy nation, His own special people, that you may proclaim the praises of Him who called you out of darkness into His mar-

velous light; who once were not a people but are now the people of God, who had not obtained mercy but now have obtained mercy."

1 Peter 2:15, 17: "For this is the will of God, that by doing good you may put to silence the ignorance of foolish men:... Honor all people. Love the brotherhood. Fear God. Honor the king."

1 Peter 4:7: "But the end of all things is at hand; therefore be serious and watchful in your prayers."

1 Peter 4:13–17: "But rejoice to the extent that you partake of Christ's sufferings, that when His glory is revealed, you may also be glad with exceeding joy. If you are reproached for the name of Christ, blessed are you, for the Spirit of glory and of God rests upon you. On their part He is blasphemed, but on your part He is glorified. But let none of you suffer as a murderer, a thief, an evildoer, or as a busybody in other people's matters. Yet if anyone suffers as a Christian, let him not be ashamed, but let him glorify God in this matter. For the time has come for judgment to begin at the house of God; and if it begins with us first, what will be the end of those who do not obey the gospel of God?"

1 Peter 5:8–9: "Be sober, be vigilant; because your adversary the devil walks about like a roaring lion, seeking whom he may devour. Resist him, steadfast in the faith, knowing that the same sufferings are experienced by your brotherhood in the world."

2 Peter 1:2–8: "Grace and peace be multiplied to you in the knowledge of God and of Jesus our Lord, as His divine power has given to us all things that pertain to life and godliness, through the knowledge of Him who called us by glory and virtue, by which have been given to us exceedingly great and precious promises, that through these you may be partakers of the divine nature, having escaped the corruption that is in the world through lust. But also for this very reason, giving all diligence, add to your faith virtue, to virtue knowledge, to knowledge self-control, to self-control perseverance, to perseverance godliness, to godliness brotherly kindness, and to brotherly kindness love. For if these things are yours and abound, you will be neither barren nor unfruitful in the knowledge of our Lord Jesus Christ."

Jude 20–23: "But you, beloved, building yourselves up on your most holy faith, praying in the Holy Spirit, keep yourselves in the love of God, looking for the mercy of our Lord Jesus Christ unto eternal life. And on some have compassion, making a distinction; but others save with fear, pulling them out of the fire, hating even the garment defiled by the flesh."

Jude 24–25: "Now to Him who is able to keep you from stumbling, and to present you faultless before the presence of His glory with exceeding joy, to God our Savior, Who alone is wise, be glory and majesty, dominion and power, both now and forever. Amen."

PRAYER FOR SALVATION AND BAPTISM OF HOLY SPIRIT

Father God in heaven,

I admit I have done wrong. I admit I have sinned and need your forgiveness, grace, and mercy. I come before you to fully confess my sins. (Name each sin specifically if possible, and name sinful activities specifically.) I believe and accept what Jesus did on the cross for me—taking my sins upon Himself and willingly substituting Himself for me—and I accept the free gift of forgiveness and eternal life that He offers me. I ask that you forgive me and wash away all my sins by the blood that Jesus shed for me. I ask for Your grace and empowerment by Holy Spirit to break the power and attraction of these sins in my life. I never want to commit these sins again. Father, I believe that I have been fully forgiven, cleansed, and empowered to behave the way You desire. Thank you!

Father, in the name of Jesus, I now come against any and all demonic spirits that may have become attached to me, inside or outside of me, as a result of my involvement in sin and sinful activities, generational curses, any and all word curses, or by any other means. I break agreement with all demonic spirits. I confess and fully renounce all authority and agreement I may have made with them, whether by consent or in ignorance. I declare that I have been washed clean with the blood of Jesus, my Lord and Savior, and I fully belong to my Father God in heaven. I now plead the blood of Jesus against each and every demonic spirit. Your legal rights to me have now been broken. Every doorway of entrance into my life is now closed in the name of Jesus, and I seal each access point shut with the blood of Jesus. Demons, I command you in the name of my Lord and Savior,

213

Jesus Christ, to leave me right now and never come back! I command you to go! I command this in the name of Jesus Christ!

Father, I thank you that I am fully cleansed, saved, and born again. I believe that all my sins have been forgiven and that I am totally clean and free by the power of the name and blood of Jesus Christ. Thank you! I now turn my entire life over to you, giving you my body, soul, and spirit, my mind, will, and emotions. I place all that I am in Your hands, trusting You from this point on for all aspects of my life. I ask for the baptism of Holy Spirit, the infilling of Holy Spirit, to enter my soul. I admit my need for my comforter, my advisor, my teacher, the spirit of truth to be inside me and alongside of me to guide and teach me to live according to Your truth. I now accept the free gift of baptism of Holy Spirit. I believe that I have now received it. I ask for the evidence of speaking in tongues to manifest in my life. I willingly yield my mind and mouth to Holy Spirit as part of this manifestation. I also ask for an impartation of Your love for others, that I might exhibit the love of Jesus in my life. I praise You and thank You for these gifts, in Jesus's name. Amen.

ABOUT THE AUTHOR

Margaret Pogin grew up in a western suburb of Chicago, Illinois. One of her favorite things as a child was a porcelain music box shaped like an open Bible with the Lord's prayer written across the two open pages. Growing up in a difficult family situation, she often thought about escaping and walking to her grandfather's farm in Missouri where she knew she was loved. She wanted to be like her grandfather who read the Bible every day.

She was painfully shy as a child. One vivid memory of this shyness is of wanting to eat the graham cracker her Sunday School teacher placed in front of her at snack time. She was so shy, though, that she couldn't bring herself to lift her head or move her hand to get the cracker. She also developed asthma and was required to stay indoors the reduce exposure to the pollens. To help keep her quiet, her mother signed her up for a book club. Margaret devoured those books and became an avid reader. She read through the entire biography section in her grade school library and then worked her way through most of the rest of the books before moving on to high school.

Margaret worked on the high school eight-page weekly newspaper and became a feature writer of the center section, which was a two-page in-depth piece on a special topic each week. She went on to graduate from Northwestern University, Evanston, Illinois, with a degree in public address and group communications as well as a degree in music history.

She was introduced to her husband, Rich, as a blind date for New Year's Eve, by a mutual friend. They were married four months later, residing in Minnesota. Together they started their own company in the financial planning industry. From there, they branched out and formed other companies and commercial real estate ventures until they retired.

After her first trip to Israel where she received the baptism of Holy Spirit, Margaret became the leader of the Ladies ministry in her local church. She served in many capacities within the church. She also served as a teacher in children's ministry, adult Sunday School, as well as teaching adults in special classes in the sanctuary. She was also a speaker at local women's meetings and retreats. She also was very involved with local as well as state-wide prayer meetings.

Her church offered a training course in chaplaincy. Upon completion of that basic course as well as a domestic abuse special training chaplaincy course, she was invited to join a Prison Fellowship Bible study at the nearby maximum-security women's prison. She served on that team for five years before she and her husband retired and moved to Florida.

Settling into the local church in Florida, she continued speaking at women's events and teaching various adult classes with her husband. She has preached in the local church as well as several times internationally. She currently leads the women's intercessory prayer group at her church in Florida.

Margaret and her husband have been married forty-three years. They have four children and currently four grandchildren.